MANY LESSONS OF LIFE

*A true recall of my life, from miracles to
losses, trying my best but learning what was
better, and what success really means*

JERRY TEMPLETON

 FriesenPress

Suite 300 - 990 Fort St
Victoria, BC, V8V 3K2
Canada

www.friesenpress.com

ISBN
978-1-5255-7221-0 (Hardcover)
978-1-5255-7222-7 (Paperback)
978-1-5255-7223-4 (eBook)

1. BIOGRAPHY & AUTOBIOGRAPHY, PERSONAL MEMOIRS

Distributed to the trade by The Ingram Book Company

PRELUDE

I thank GOD for the life He has allowed me to live, along with my wife, family and friends, and all of the persons, that have helped me through life, with all it's ups and downs. Everyone is given opportunity to make decisions, right or wrong, and sometimes, you just need help to come out on the right side of life, even when you make wrong choices. Life is a series of lessons, and if we learn from them, it usually will prove for the better, and many times, we don't even realize we are in the middle of learning one, until later. Any one of us, through circumstances of life, could be down and out, on the wrong side of the law, or even worse, and we need to come to the realization, "But for the Grace of GOD, go I!"

It is my hope, this book, will help improve your life, as you understand, the lessons, I have realized, through mine.

CHAPTER 1

A number of years ago, I watched an Larry King Live interview on television, with Donald Trump. When asked about all the CEO's getting caught for ripping companies off, and ending up in jail, he replied, most of them were probably like that right from the beginning, probably even in college. They most likely got away with smaller crooked dealings and as time went on, just got more greedy, until instead of hundreds of dollars, then thousands, they were doing millions, or hundreds of millions worth of illegal deals. So when they got caught the only thing different was, the deals were bigger. Well, he figured, once you are rotten, you would most likely, always be rotten! While that is true in the most cases, there can be an exception. I am that exception! But, don't get me wrong, I am far from perfect, a long way, but, I am also a work in process, and for that I am truly thankful.

I have always said, if you are going to be crooked, mean and dishonest, why bother being just a bit that way, you might as well be the worst possible case around, because the penalty is the same. I was raised by a Christian mother, and a dad that did not want to openly admit God had any place in his life, but wouldn't say He didn't either. I was a good kid, overly busy, mom said, and most would have used different words to describe my enthusiasm for life, although it did make her creative, in coming up with measures to deal with me. Thank goodness they hadn't invented "Ritalin" yet. Mom taught us not to fight, period. I wasn't a trouble maker, just didn't back down from it, and more times than not, I could convince someone else to do the wrong thing, leaving me somewhat innocent, at least in my eyes.

One day, walking home from elementary school, on a rainy day, this bigger guy, taking advantage of the common knowledge that I would turn the other cheek, pushed me over my limit, by shoving me down into a big mud puddle. That did it! I came out swinging, and let him have all of my energy, in the form of anger, and ended up hurting him, and chipping his new front tooth. Later, that made me feel pretty bad, but after all, he started it. I was smaller, but I ended it. We ended up friends after that day, or should I say after getting it from his and my parents. I think my dad was actually proud, that I beat up the bully of the day, even though, I had to go through moms explanation, of why it was the wrong thing to do. That was the first time I realized, that, if I gave my whole effort in a fight, it would most likely be better that the other person could produce. I remember a guy up the street, breaking his two front teeth on my fist later on, and I felt guilty but on the other hand, felt good because I was smaller than most kids, and underneath had a tough streak in me.

As I grew older, I determined that whatever you did in life you had to give it 100% or why bother. That is what I did! One hundred percent was the answer!

I remember riding home for Christmas, with some guys I went to College with in Kelowna BC, about a five hour drive from home. This tough guy, sitting in the front seat, whom I didn't like too much to begin with, was harassing me as I sat in the back. Sometime during the drive, he finally pushed the wrong buttons and after not heeding my threat, I stuck my cigarette in his ear. I mean butted it! The next fifteen minutes could be described, as somewhat hectic, as six guys driving along at fifty miles per hour, through a windy highway, erupted into a struggle of the fittest, and being a bit smaller gave me a definite advantage. The car finally made it to the safety of the shoulder of the road, and as all piled out the fight was on, but by then there were more hands involved, due to all the misdirected swinging going on during the stopping process, and no one in the front seat knew, until later, what exactly happened. They didn't see the cigarette, and all they knew was, driving along, half asleep and bored by the drive, and not the least bit interested in the argument going on, suddenly, everything went ballistic. That was how I felt at that time in my life, and being good really never had a great bearing on my activities, and, as long as it didn't involve police, it was OK.

Nothing in my life during that time, could I say, I was proud of. I stayed out all night, went to work hung over many times, and many days, had to go outside at work during the morning to throw-up, enough to get through the day, and at five o'clock, start all over again. Freedom, it was called! Somehow, and I am not very clear on how it ever worked out that way, I met a girl, that saw something more in me, wanted to marry me, and a year and a half later, two weeks before my twenty-first birthday, we were wed, and that changed my life for the better, much better! Somehow it gave me a direction for my life, a future and oh yes, that 100% thing kicked in. Family, work, play, all at 100%, and if you knew me then, you might have it thought more like 150%. I channeled all my energy, which I always seemed to have a lot off, towards family, and especially work, no, money to be more exact. I came up with the idea, that a dollar today was worth one hundred dollars tomorrow and so on.

Two years after marriage, one daughter, and very little money later, we needed a larger place to live, so we looked at buying an old used house. Everything was set for me to sign the papers that day, and I only had five hundred dollars to my name, but it didn't sit right for me to buy that house, and I am not sure why. So instead of going to sign the deal, I took a drive through our town, and low and behold, found two houses in 1972, with "FOR SALE BY BUILDER" on them. So I went inside and found the builder, working alone to finish his houses. The house was ready for carpets and the market was not very great, so I listened to him go on about how he had bought the two lots and both were at the same stage of completion, and there were a number of lots he could buy if he could just sell them both. He was asking $20,500 each, which was lower than most others.

Well, I told him my situation, all about my small family, my drive to sign the papers, and then made him an offer that he ended up taking, much to his surprise. I told him I would give him $1000 more than he wanted, which would allow him to sell the house next door for $1000 more also. I explained how he could make more than he figured, and sell one of them that day, on the spot, with a hand shake. He was bewildered at first, but now was the time to use my expertise I had gained from childhood, selling something this time, an idea, to someone that had no idea that he wanted it, at least not at first. He would have a sale, give me $500 cash for a down payment, give me $500 for appliances, and everyone would be happy, and the best part, he could sell the other house for $1000 more and not give them any money at all, because nothing was on paper. The deal was done, on the spot, selling price , $ 21,500! He got a sale, and I got a down payment, something I didn't have until that moment. Within months, the property in that block doubled in price and within four years, doubled again in value. By the time I was thirty-one years old, we had paid off our house, truck, new car, new travel trailer, and had money in the bank.

Those years were good to us. We danced and partied every weekend, traveled to other countries every winter as a couple, usually with friends, and always took our kids camping, even if it was just for the day or weekend, but very often. I worked as many hours as my bosses wanted me to and never ever turned down extra hours, no matter what the weather, because I always felt, there was always someone that would be willing to take my opportunity to make money out of my hands. And so I applied the two ideas, give 100% and one dollar today was worth one hundred dollars tomorrow, and you know what, it worked then and still does today, even for getting out of debt or putting your money back into your business to make it more stable and debt free. During those years, I also realized, most of the men I worked with were not business minded, but most were just good men trying to make a decent living. That was a big opening for me, of learning how to sell myself and my way of thinking, to them. I would take charge of everything, every job, every situation, even though, I was scared myself a few times, of overstepping my boundaries. But I always supported the guys around me in a positive way, convincing them they were doing better and working hard to improve their skills, so they could do more jobs under me, which got them better pay and made me look as if I knew what I was doing.

From the beginning, men older that myself, trusted me and stuck behind me, at least most of the time. There always will be a few that just don't see the big picture along with those that are not good at much, but I found through life, another key to success. Everyone has something to give, and the sooner you could find that something, and get them working on it, they would do better, feel better, and trust you from then on, and when you might need them, they would be there for you. I don't know if it is just my thinking, or lots of us think that way, but it seems most people in their jobs, shouldn't be. They cause others so much grief, just because they are unqualified at the position they hold, while at the same time, afraid to take good ideas from those around them, that only want to help them? Too many, think suggestions, are really criticism of their abilities, rather than free advice, from another point of view. A good boss or manager, takes all the advice they can get, and uses some of it and discards the rest, and if your can supply ideas to help, you are usually promoted for it, sooner or later. And that is what I did, a lot of! I discovered, most of the men I worked for, did not have a great education, didn't have really good communication skills, and certainly seemed to lack the ability to run a company, let alone manage the employees. I just always tried to figure out, the best, cheapest, but most effective ways to do the job at hand, and, I had the imagination, my mother didn't know how to control. I soon discovered, applied in the right place, it could get me top job, no matter where or what I was doing.

Shortly after our first child was born, I was working as a lead hand, for a fabricating company, that built just about anything you wanted, but got into building feed mills, hoppers, augers and construction equipment. I used my gusto for life, to turn into, "I can do anything you want and build anything you need", much to the delight of the owner, who was just a farmer, trying to build a business that he saw a demand for. We took on jobs that no one else even wanted, working in any conditions, anywhere, to survive. And we did! I watched how much money we made on each job, and, as I seemed to be a strong part of the "doing" part of the company, I would ask for raises, on a successful job basis. It worked pretty good, as, without me, he would have trouble continuing to make the same progress. At least that was my take on it, and he seemed to go along with it. Up until then, I had been working, through the Union, on construction jobs, but they had all slowed down, and this seemed to be right down my alley.

One day, about eight months after starting work for the fabricating company, I got a call from the Union dispatcher, telling me to leave the next day, for a road construction camp, a twelve hour drive away. As I didn't want to get into trouble with the Union, I informed my boss, the owner, and, the next day, headed to the job. I was pretty upset about leaving my young family, but, I needed the union job and felt it was my only choice. Due to road delays, I arrived at the camp, in the middle of nowhere, late at night, and, was shown into a bunkhouse room, that had a drunken construction worker, snoring like nothing I had ever heard before. I never slept all night, and 5 am was up for breakfast and off to work. Or so I thought. The foreman, sent me to work with another heavy duty mechanic, and we drove here and there and did nothing all day. Absolutely nothing, for twelve hours. They told me that was the best part about this job, because is was so spread out, you really never saw anyone or did anything productive, but got paid big money. I though to myself, the next day would be better, but, it was more of the same. In talking to some of the other men, I understood, there was not much work available anywhere, so, they would make sure this job would go on for years, and it did, but I didn't. Sunday morning, on the third day there, I went to my Foreman, and told him I QUIT, and as far as I was concerned, I didn't even want to get paid for the twenty-four hours I had worked for the company, because I didn't do anything, and neither did anyone else. And I drove the twelve hours home! I had tears, most of the way home, sad for passing up this good pay, knowing I had let the Union down, wondering if I had a job to go back to back home, but most of all, missing my girls! That was one tough drive back. Not having had much sleep, and worried sick about what lie ahead for me, but at the same time, just never wanting to be put in that position again, of having to choose between, my family or my work. After that, I never had to leave my family, for other than short times, but always a predetermined amount of time, away. Good lesson in how valuable my family was to me!

On returning, I went back to work, building feed mills and many more things, over the next few years, and eventually, building a gravel pit, complete with belts, gravel screening and washing plant and crushers. When it was completed, I got a big break! I was offered, and accepted a job helping to operate it, with a Union Company, that appreciated my hard work ethics. I never looked back after that, as my work spoke volumes of my abilities.

CHAPTER 2

I worked most of my life as a union worker, not always in agreement with their policies but for the most part, supportive. I was always trying to give my best and trying to get the best out of my fellow workers, so the employer would be satisfied he had the best quality for his buck, and also trying to get the employees to feel proud for doing a great job. Most of the time that was the case, but early on I encountered a few problems and later it would prove to almost change my life forever, and not to the good. The first time I went to work for a big company, at their request, I found out I was not welcome. They wanted me because I had experience with repairing heavy earth moving machinery. They bought bulldozers, earth movers, and front end loaders and had bid some road building jobs, as that is the direction they felt the economy was moving.

I was the youngest guy in the place, and on the second day on the job, Gerry, a fellow worker which had worked for the company for a number of years, if one chose to call it work, came over, introduced himself and shook my hand, and walked away. That told him something about me, that would have an "x" beside my name from then on with that company, which you will soon understand. I was only thirty years old, and the three men working under me were all ten years or more my senior, but that didn't bother me, because I had full confidence in my ability and supported them all, in their learning process concerning this upcoming road construction equipment. I had a deadline to meet and I was hustling and working alongside these guys, to meet it. Not three weeks on the job, Gerry, cornered me out in the yard, and told me I had better slow down, because I was making the rest of them look bad, and if I knew what was good for me, this conversation never happened, and he was serious! That caught me by surprise, and for the next few hours, I was pretty shook up, as I didn't know what I should do. I knew already there was some kind of inside link between Gerry and the main office management, that was in the next building about 100 yards from the complex we worked in and out of. My boss was in our building, which controlled all the work in the shop and the yard, and across in the main office, were the company head management with the CEO and all the engineers, supervisors and support staff, which controlled all of the provincial work. They were heavy into refineries, pipelines, crane work and always bidding new jobs. They controlled the pipe building part of the company that had a good piece of the market share. Gerry was a professional at doing nothing, always having to go get something, or check on something, but never doing much of anything, and

JERRY TEMPLETON

never getting in any kind of trouble for it, and it was very obvious. I noticed him going into the head office on a number of occasions, and there was no reason I could think of, for him to go there.

There were a couple of other things about him that stood out, and as I had been threatened, I took note of any strange actions of the person that threatened me. He would be at work long before anyone else, and stay after everyone had gone, and he was always checking his oil or tires or something on his pickup or car in the work yard, not in the parking lot like normal employees. I would come in early and leave late, just to make him uncomfortable, and sometimes leave at the end of the day and then come back as if I forgot something. Well, I discovered a pile of Company tools, out in the yard, in a box of used oil cans, under the cans, as if someone had done a job and forgot the tools there. The only problem was, with the wrenches were some expensive measuring tools that would never be used in any application in that area. So I watched the box, stayed late, and in the morning , came in one hour early, parked in a different area and went out in the yard, to make sure the tools were still there, and just watched. Sure enough, Gerry, drove up, opened his hood, and without even looking around, took a can of oil from his truck, put some in his engine, put the can in the box, and put the box, tools and all, in his truck, and drove out to his parking spot. Later on that day, I confronted Gerry about what he did, while the evidence was in his truck, in the employees lot, and found just where, I fit in the food chain. He was not concerned for the least bit, in fact he laughed at me and let me know as a matter of fact, I was not a "mason", the "x" beside my name, and had no right here, and if I made a scene, not to count on the support from head office, because he had already communicated about me to them. He said I didn't fit, but everyone would help me get the equipment ready so I could be shipped out to the job with it. I left the discussion and went to my boss and told him what had transpired. He just sat there and listened until I was done, and then told me, he knew I was doing a bang up job, but, Gerry was right, I didn't fit, and I was here for a purpose, so do my job and shut up or I would end up losing it in the end. He told me there was a relationship between Gerry and higher up management that I didn't want to know about. It took me until a couple of years later to find out what that was. A number of the management, had been working together on a new mine site, finishing their contract, when, Gerry had discovered the results of the core samples, before it was public knowledge, while on the site late one night, and told them! As a result, they all bought shares in the mine shortly before it opened and before the info was released, and the shares went up, and, they all made some big money. So they owed him and took care of him because of it!

I left with the equipment a few months later, as Master Mechanic, on a ten million dollar job, which ended up over eighteen million, with lots of extra work added on, over two years. That is where I really found out what being a mason to that group of men really meant. After the first year, and working in tough conditions, seven days a week, operating twenty-four hours a day, my crews had their work cut out for them, and they did a fantastic job. As I was a stickler for keeping track of everything and everyone under my supervision, I kept extensive records of inventories, as we were a ways from any town and a day from supplies. Going into our first winter, with everything going great, I was surprised when I got informed by the Job superintendent, I had help coming in the form of a older gentleman, John, that would be around to help keep things flowing smooth through the end of the job, mainly because his other site was done and head office wanted him kept employed. I accepted the explanation and felt I could give him some responsibilities that would free up some of my time for other duties.

We were using the heaviest steel cutting edges and teeth on the equipment that was available, and in the night time, the sparks would fly, even in the rain as the metal tore at the rock. These steel cutting edges and teeth, were put on the blades and buckets of heavy equipment, so they would wear during impact with the ground so as not to damage the machine itself. They were attached with bolts or pins for easy replacement. Three inch thick steel cutting edges on the caterpillars, which would normally last a week, would need to be changed, every eight hour shift, at a cost of approximately $800 a piece. We had a stockyard full of the teeth and cutting edges, and I kept records of every change and every piece that went out, myself. We had estimated $300,000/year on this ground engaging steel so it was important to me to keep track of the usage, even for calculating future jobs. I made a habit of stopping and checking the inventory of steel every night before leaving, and through our maintenance control, knew what would go out every night. I could check in the morning to make sure the parts were changed as required, otherwise damage to equipment would occur.

Within a week, this older guy, John, came along, and the first time we met, we shook hands, and he looked at me funny for a moment, and asked "You are not a Mason"? He could tell because of a special handshake they developed to help recognize another Mason. I responded that I didn't know what he meant, so he informed me Mason's were a group of men, that worked together to raise money for different charity organizations, and, they made it a priority, to take care of one another, no matter what, and he could get me into the Order, so I would never have a problem staying employed. I told him we would have to discuss it at a later date. He then went on about a representative from the cutting edge company, that was on his last job, that would be going past the job site every week due to his job demands. Starting the following week, this salesman would deliver any steel we needed, as he was going by anyway, so we could save on freight costs. I had no reason to suspect anything, assuming it would help to save money. It took me a while to catch on to their plan. Usually I left for dinner around 6pm and would come back to check on everything at around 800 pm, then leave for the night between 10 and 11pm to return at 630 the next morning. John was living in a trailer in town, and I would drive by it every night on my way out and many nights I would see the sales mans truck parked there in the evening. John told me, sometimes he would end up coming through earlier that planned and they would have a few drinks together before he went to his motel for the night. To save the salesman a trip, in the morning, John would bring up the steel parts in his company truck, along with the bills, and unload them in plain site, outside of the inventory compound. There was a call for snow one night and when we left the worksite, the flakes were coming down pretty good. When I got there in the morning there was only about two inches covering everything, except where some cutting edges had been, leaving some bare spots where they once sat. Without missing a beat, I knew those pieces should not have needed replacing, so I noted the missing parts in my log and continued the day. It wasn't long, before John showed up, and low and behold, he had brought some stock up for the salesman, that just so happened to be exactly the same ones that were missing, from the bare spots in the snow. That is when I knew there was something crooked going on. It took me a few weeks of tracking all the cutting edges, along with tracking John and the sales man's meetings, which even including sneaking into John's trailer park at night, to check what was in his truck. The snowfall, off and on through the winter, helped to determine the movement of parts between the two of them, but I finally had it all documented. John would pick up the pieces from the compound at night, take them home with him, and in the morning, return with a bill for new ones and the pieces he took, basically selling us our own inventory over and over. I had found a stack of the suppliers new billing papers in John's pickup glove compartment some months earlier, and kept one copy from the stack as evidence.

Finally, I had enough of this fiasco, and John, and as the weather changed and spring was coming, the job got extremely busy and I just could not trust John any more. I went to my site boss, the project superintendent, and told him of the extra costs that were occurring and explained about the fraud I believed to be happening.

He said he would address the issue and I left it at that. A couple of days later, I got a call from head office, asking for me to report to the head of my department, a man that I only met with every couple of months. I figured something was happening regarding John, so, I packed up all my documentation I had accumulated regarding him, and made the three hour trip. When I got there, I was ushered into to his office, and sat and listened to him explain, how happy he was with the job I was doing, and informed me they were bidding some more rather large, similar jobs and would like me to come back to head office to work there, so I would be available when needed through the bidding process. About halfway through this discussion, my heart sank in my chest, as I realized I was being removed from the job site, due to the fraud by John. At the end of the discussions, I asked for a letter that would state my change in job position, that I could take back to show the job superintendent, when I went to retrieve my files from that job site. I waited while he had it drafted, and then after he gave it to me I left and got in my truck, and headed back to the job, feeling sick inside about what just happened. He never did want to see the documentation I had collected, even though I showed him the stack of papers and described what was going on, and how it was costing the company thousands of dollars a month. He simply stated he would take care of it, so I figured he knew all about it and most likely had his finger in the pie. I only drove a little ways, and pulled over and contemplated what had just happened, and how it could effect my future in the industry.

After sizing up the situation, and believing I had nothing to lose, I turned around, went back to head office, and went up to the President's office. I had only met him very briefly on two occasions, and both events were superficial, so I felt a bit intimidated but also felt I was wronged, and believed if I left, all my work was for naught, and the story would somehow be twisted to undermine my abilities. I waited for about an hour, but finally he allowed me in. Once there I wasted no time explaining what had just happened, and showed him all the evidence I had collected. I felt from the start, I was doing the right thing, and felt from him, he was genuinely concerned and would actually do something. At the conclusion of the meeting, he told me to go back to the job, leave the company truck there, collect my belongings, and go home for the week. I had been with the company for almost 3 years, and given 100%, not to mention, I had earned very good money. Within a few days, I received a call from another company, and the union office, and was instructed to report to work for this new company, closer to home. Apparently, the President had recommended to this new Company's Owner, his friend, they hire me due to my excellent record of employment and abilities. That would prove to be a twelve year, exciting run, with huge responsibility, during which, it would create a turning point in my life, that would impact me forever. Shortly after I left, I was told, the President, fired the head manager of equipment in head office, along with the project Superintendent, and none other than crooked John. I understood, an investigation followed that led to fraud charges through that department, so they all got what was coming to them. GREED!! And if uncontrolled, it will get you, sooner, or later!

CHAPTER 3

I started working for this new company, as a heavy duty mechanic and soon after as Master Mechanic, which, was the supervisor over the mechanics and repairs of all the equipment on a job site. It seemed through life, my aggressive nature, always put me in charge, no matter what I was doing, and most times I would be younger that all of the men under me, but that never really created any problem. I found most men in construction, although doing their best, were never educated or trained enough to give them the confidence they needed to take charge and be able to handle the paperwork it required. Another factor, was, they were never offered training, to keep up with the ever changing technology. Oh, there was some training course offered from time to time, but usually to those out of work, so they would get a bit of income, but the men who really needed it, were never out of work, so, the only training, was anything provided on the job. The guys that were working, all came from the school of hard knocks, or so it seemed. A few of them came from friend-ships and through working with a growing company since inception. I got along with those individuals that tried or worked hard, and occasionally had friction with those that didn't. So guys would soon know where they fit with me, as I made no bones about it. I guess that is what management saw in me, and appreciated, I always had the company's best interest in mind, even if it did cause friction occasionally, the bottom line, I was always company. After six years working for them, and proving my dedication, I had the respect of my superiors.

I should go back a couple of years, just so you can understand how I gained some serious respect. In con-struction, there is always someone trying to do you in or trying to undermine your authority and in some cases, enjoy to see you caught up in something that causes your demise. People lived on coffee, cigarettes and booze, and that always gave rise to schemes and rumors. That was every day, latest news to keep things interesting, so over my life in the industry, I heard or saw just about anything you could imagine, and worked hard to keep from being distracted. I always set myself a short term and a long range goal, with deadlines, so as not to be distracted from meeting them.

I was sent to a construction job in northern British Columbia, after a job that had just started. The project superintendent, fired everyone, due to the remote loca-tion, booze, and peoples lack of ability to handle such a large project. I was sent in to re-establish a maintenance crew and program under extreme conditions. When I arrived, I found out the Project Superintendent, my new boss, was an old navy man, that thought he was running a ship, and that is exactly what he did. He was the toughest but the best thing that ever happened to me in construction, and I was a sponge to his techniques and business smarts. He let me know the first day, that unless I was willing to sacrifice, and give 150%, I might as well leave now. He promised, if I ever "BS'ed" him, or mislead him, in any way, he would hang me, and I believe, looking back, he would have. He was tough as nails, so you always knew where you stood, but he was smart like a fox, and was construction savvy, and always one step ahead of everyone else. The company originally went in with a twenty million dollar contract and left with sixty million worth of work. At the twenty million level we would have lost a fortune due to the severe winter and tough conditions, not to mention the costs of moving in all the equipment and support trailers. The temperatures in summer cruised to102 F and in winter -40F and severe winds. We supplied concrete right through the winter, using steam, boiling water and chemicals in the trucks, combined with pouring it in huge air blown, insulated tents, that covered two acres of worksite. Outside the tent, the steel equipment would just snap in pieces. All the machinery had to run twenty-four hours a day, seven days a week, for the entire cold spell, and if they broke down, we would put cargo parachutes over them and startup huge diesel hot air blowers under them, to warm them up enough, in order to be able to restart them again. None of us had ever experienced that kind of extreme, and probably never will again. In the winter, you could not have exposed skin due to cold, and summertime you didn't want exposed skin due to bugs. The costs skyrocketed with each cold spell, but not only for us, but for the other contractors on site also, and the government, who had a deadline to meet. Well, that fox of a Super I was under, knew it would result in more dollars for all the extra's, and he was right again. We would bid on every extra work that came along, and after I would put my bid together, I would report to him, he would glance at it, ask me what the profit margin was, then instruct me to quadruple it, submit it, and not to budge on the price. We got everything we put in for. There were one thousand men in this remote camp, well fed and full of liquor ever night. So there was nowhere for extra persons to be brought into, if they wanted lower bid prices, and no more hours to be worked, without paying the huge overtime and housing costs.

So the lesson of supply and demand took on a whole new light for me. I learned, that if you worked to control the marketplace, you could dictate your prices, no matter where you were, or what you did. Until now, I had only needed to sell myself to others, but through this job, I learned some skill of selling to companies that were desperate to meet their deadlines, another valuable lesson that I would use later in life. The job was a huge success, and for my perseverance, I was not only rewarded financially, during a poor time in the economy for everyone else, I was respected by my peers in the company, and would always hold a job position. Years later, due to the health of the owner, we had an auction of all the equipment in order to shut the company down, and out of it another small company was formed by some of the management, and I was included to help run that entity until the time came for me to move on and work towards and succeed in having my own business. It was all just stepping stones to my own success. The learning curve, was rewarding, due to tough conditions, keeping the goal in sight, and saving to be set up financially, which in construction is referred to as, talking back money. We now had no bills at all and a chunk of cash in the bank, getting 20% interest at that time.

During the time I was away, working long hours and putting big cash in the bank, the rest of the country, was in a depression. There were not a lot of jobs around, and house prices were falling, interest rates rising, and many people we knew, lost their homes, due to inability to make their mortgage payments. Many had bought real estate, at 30 to 50% higher than it was worth on the day. Just like that, jobs dried up! We had looked at a new house on a small acreage, and put in an offer $130,000 below what they were asking for it, and they laughed in our face and said if they were going to take that big of a loss, they would sell to someone in the family or in their company. One year later, the day after Christmas, we got a call to see if we were still interested in the house, as it had sat empty for the year, and any loss now could be written off. We stated the same price as one year earlier, and had the money to do the deal without subjects. Again they thought they could get more from us, but we held our ground, and before the new year, we had a deal. We sold our house, to my sister and her husband, that didn't have any options to get into their own house, and as we got a deal, we felt it only right, to give them one too. So it happened. Our plan was to keep the new place for five years, until the market recovered, and just as planned, year five, sold and pocketed over $100,000. profit, tax free. We downsized, to a new custom built home for us, that would still be new enough when we went to sell it down the road. Over the next fifteen years, we used that house as collateral, by setting up a line of credit against it, so we could use that money how and when we needed it, to allow us flexibility to get involved in business and land deals, as they came along. That way, we always would keep some cash, available in different accounts, as a safety net, should anything come along unexpected. We always worked our debt, so it was the cheapest money available, instead of a demand loan that would cost you dearly, and of course, when you needed money in a hurry, for some deal, you usually had some kind of holdup, causing missed deals.

From that time on, we always seemed to have money. When you don't need it, the financial institutes, are dying to give you some at prime rate, but if you ever really do need some, they never heard of prime rate. Any financing after that, was always worked off of prime, and that is a must. During the days we had a large chunk of cash, my wife would phone all the banks, to see who had the best interest rate, and when they found out what you had to deposit, they would suddenly change gears, along with a much improved rate, to get your money in. It still works like that today. They make very good returns on your money, while it is in their vaults, so they don't have a problem, giving you a "special" deal. On the other side of the coin, the poor victim that has to borrow, pays double or more, of what they offer on a deposit. That's how the rich get richer, simple math.

Back to the early thoughts, that proved to be true. A dollar today, is worth a hundred tomorrow. I do not know why I figured it out so early in my life, because they never taught us anything about inflation in school, but maybe it was because, I tended to be smart and quick when it came to math and numbers. A lesson that still hold true today.

CHAPTER 4

A couple of years later, this new company focus was to only bid jobs over 50 million dollars, and sure enough we landed a good job only a couple of hours from home, that would take two years of my life, and almost all of it. The first year went great, with lots of earth moving, rock work, crushing and bridge construction. We had day and night shifts throughout the job, with everyone working a considerable amount of overtime all year. The new construction saw lots of drug use, something you never saw much of until then. Our company had another large project, nine hours further away from us, that, during the first winter, had to be shut down due to winter conditions for four months. So they shipped down a large amount of their equipment, along with the Superintendent and some of his "henchmen". They didn't click very good with us, as they knew they had to leave, so they didn't put much effort into our job. To them it was more like putting in time and telling us how we should be doing everything different. They also realized, our job site was closer to home, and head office and that theirs would be finished in a few months, but we had another year of work. Our management team discussed the problems they were creating and felt it best to tough it out and they would leave. They did, but they came back. While they were with us, they had been spending their time undermining everything we were doing, in their communications with head office. When they returned in early summer, on completion of their project, unfortunately, our Project Superintendent, became seriously ill, and ended up in the hospital and then at home recovering for some time. Seeing how we now had a Super from the other job available, he stepped in, and wasted no time doing it. He brought his right hand Master Mechanic, and informed me to split my authority and workload with him. He was arrogant and useless from the get go, and didn't have a problem communicating to me that my days were numbered.

The new Super, tried everything to undermine my ability and even had head office wondering about me. My part of the job was going fine until then, and suddenly my costs started going through the roof, and every time I turned around, the other Master was ordering all sorts of specialty parts and extra inventory, which I challenged him over. It just got worse as time went on, with lots of management meetings happening without my knowledge. From the start I could see the plan unfold and I communicated my concerns with the President of the company, with whom I had a good relationship, due to my previous record. He explained he understood and though sympathetic insisted I persevere, as he had no one else to Super the job at this time. Within seven weeks, he called me into head office and asked me to step down as Master mechanic on that job site, but he would prefer I stay there and work along side my crew for the duration of the job. That was a tough request, but after his assurance that my job was secure with the company, I agreed to stay there, as tough as it would be. I returned to a position that would keep me inside, away from most of the construction operations, but still available to help the company through the project. It was a slam to my ego, and I kept hearing all the rumors coming from the Super, of my incompetence leading up to my demotion. To say I was fuming would be an understatement. I hated his guts!! And as every day started and finished, it ,ate me up, more and more, until I couldn't even sleep at night. I was a mess and I knew it and He knew it, and he would walk by me and look at me like I was a sick dog and should be put out of my misery. That is just what I felt like too!

I voiced my frustration to more than a few people, and one day one of them came to me and mentioned, they knew someone that would take care of my problem, if I wanted to bad enough. I wanted to hear more. I was informed that this certain someone was actually a professional hit man, and for a small fee, would take care of the Super, no questions asked. Ya right I though to myself,but the more I listened to how this guy operated, the more I thought it might be a possibility, even a probability. I thought about it for a week, all the time fuming more and more, thinking I would get even and this was the only way. I asked to meet this guy and within a week, I did, in a parking lot, in a normal place in this small town and we talked. I met a guy, a couple of years older than myself, a bit taller, with pot marks in a hard face, that was totally professional and at the same time, showing no feelings one way or another. He left me with a coldness! This was his job and he had no problem with it. I would not have to be concerned about any possibility of anyone, connecting me to the demise of the person I wanted gone. It would be an accident, just like the many accidents that happen every day, at least that was what it would look like. We only spent maybe a few minutes together, and I got a phone number to call. It was just that simple! I went on my way, believing I had found the answer to my problem, not even concerned about the Super, only that I would win in the end, and he would lose! Big time!!

I remember, thinking of the time, in a split second, I came within inches of being killed instantly, on my first big construction job. We were building a new road, 500 to 1000 feet above the existing road, that would eventually end up flooded by a dam being constructed eight miles downstream. The job lasted six months, through spring and summer, where the temperature soared to 110 degrees with thunderstorms many nights during the summer. It was a small crew, and we worked Mondays, through the next weekend, until the next Friday night and then got Saturday and Sunday off, just to start all over again on Monday. When I got off on Friday at about 6:00 pm, I would drive six hours home, at about sixty to seventy miles per hour, well over the speed limit, so I would be home around midnight. I would sleep until 9 am and then my young daughters would jump on me to wake me and love me to pieces. For a week in mid summer, they came to the job where they got to stay in a trailer beside the crew quarters, and had the french pastry chef, cook special treats for them in the middle of the day, while the cookhouse was empty. We got up every morning at 5:15 am, walked one hundred feet to the cookhouse, had breakfast, made a sandwich for coffee break, and headed out to work at 6:30. We came in for lunch, went back out until 4:30 when we stopped at the work trailer, had two beers each, dinner at 6pm, and back out to work until everything was done for the morning, usually until 11:00 pm. Every day the same, but every day overtime, which was one and one-half times pay. And no time or place to spend it.

Every night, myself along with the other three mechanics, would head out to opposite ends of the job, and work to meet at the middle. We worked in pairs, as everything was manhandled and heavy going. One of our duties included checking all the fluid levels, checking for leaks and broken or loose parts and checking to see if the cutting edges and teeth on the machinery needed replacing. The equipment was always left parked in a row, so we would both start on the same machine with one guy climbing up and checking the fluid levels, then starting the machine and raise the caterpillar blade and ripper, so the other guy could see if the ground engaging tools (teeth and cutting edges), needed changing. On all the cats, the operator, when he pulled on the lever, the blade or ripper would go up, but if you hit the lever, the blade, which weighed about 10,000 pounds, would drop in a split second to the ground. On the next machine, we would switch roles so one man would not have to do all the climbing and it was the quickest procedure. One night, it wasn't dark yet, but we were nearing our weekend off, so we were pretty exhausted, and everything was going smooth. Ron, my working partner, jumped up on a D9 caterpillar, checked the oil and started it up, just as I finished the previous machine. So I walked to the front of it, and like every day, he raised the huge blade up to its limit, about thee feet above the ground, and I knelt down in front of it, put my head almost on the ground to see the underside, and in the blink of an eye, before I could move, the blade crashed full force on the ground, within twelve inches of my nose. It was so sudden, I was frozen in time, without even breathing, and then I thought of Ron. I knew he was sitting in the operators seat, thinking he had just killed me when he accidentally hit the control lever. Partly in shock and part by instinct, I jumped up, ran around the side of the blade, screaming, "I'M ALL RIGHT! ,I'M ALL RIGHT!" Poor Ronnie! He was sitting frozen in the seat, white as a ghost, and couldn't even speak. I climbed the six feet up to where he was seated, and neither of us said a thing, we just sat there, for probably five or ten minutes, before saying anything. My first words were "YOU SCARED THE LIVING SHIT OUT OF ME!" but it was more of an explanation than that of anger. He replied, still reserved in his speaking, almost quietly, "I thought I killed you"!! We both climbed down, grabbed our thermos's of ice water, took a ten minute time out ,and then as our hearts started beating back to normal, talked through what just happened and somehow thanked each other for working safe together, so we could continue as a team. It could have been a totally different night, except for a few inches, and that is how accidents happen. I never forgot about that time. Neither did Ron. I said to myself, it just wasn't my time. But it also made me realize, that, one minute you

JERRY TEMPLETON

are here, and, just that fast, in an instant, your life can be over.

Back to my option of the hit man. Over the next days, I ran the options over and over in my mind, almost oblivious to everyday life, only looking at what the future would be like if I made that phone call? Sunday came along, and I had the weekend off, so as per usual, my wife and I took our three daughters to Sunday School, as we had since they were old enough to go. When they were younger, we would drop them off and go out for coffee or breakfast, and pick them up when they were done. As they grew up, they questioned our absence from church, so, as we were both brought up in church, on Sunday, we went along with them. Anyway, this Sunday we went, and the service was basically the same as any other morning in church. I had no inkling of an idea what would happen that morning, or I don't really know if I would have gone or not. The pastor was talking about something, but I never heard one word he said, I had other things on my mind. And then, out of the blue, right while the service was going on, I heard a voice, just like there was no one in the place except me, clear as a bell, say " Jerry! You are going to get up and walk to the end of the row, and you are going to turn and go down to the front of the church, and change you life forever, or, you are going to turn and leave, and never set foot in a church again"! I wasn't even scared. It was almost like I knew that voice. It was amazing. Now, here I was, a construction worker, that had seen just about anything you could imagine, foul mouthed as the rest, not afraid of much, and definitely never ever, heard or believed in a voice from nowhere, BUT, it was that definite, and absolutely clear to me, and

I reacted almost immediately. I stood up, and sidestepped by the people on the bench, and stopped when I got to the aisle, not turning right or left, just stopped, facing the side wall of the church, pondering the question in my mind, probably frozen there for only a few seconds, and then, convinced this was real, turned left. I walked down the aisle, right in the middle of the service, all by myself, got to the bottom of the aisle and just stopped there. I can't even imagine what everyone though. The Pastor never stopped preaching, people had no idea what was going on, my wife must have had some wild thoughts go through her mind, but I knew what had happened. As I stood at the foot of the aisle, ten feet from the platform the Pastor was on, another younger Pastor, knowing something strange was happening, and obviously felt he should intervene, to save disrupting the service, made his way over to me. He whispered and asked me what I needed, and I told him I needed to get right with God, so he sat down with me, and prayed with me, that God would hear my heart and meet my need.

I sat there for the remainder of the service, and sometime, I'm not sure exactly when, my wife came and sat by my side as I wept, feeling like something had really changed, as if I could breath for the first time by myself. When the service was over, the Head Pastor came over to me, and after being briefed by the younger Pastor, put his arm over my shoulder and said a prayer, thanking God for my life, and for never giving up on me, and to help me the rest of my life, and walk with me every step of it. By now, most had left, so we gathered our kids, and went home. The drive home was very quiet, and I don't think the kids and maybe even my wife, really knew what

JERRY TEMPLETON

had just happened. But I knew, and just in case I had any doubts, God showed me something three hours later, just to prove it. I have said, it was Gods sense of humor. Three hours later, out of the blue, I suddenly realized, I hadn't had a cigarette since church, nor did I want one, nor did I miss it!! To this day, I have never craved smoking nor did I have any withdrawal symptoms. I had tried three times in my life to quit, and all three times, I was sick, hungry, nauseous and grumpy. In that moment I realized, I had quit forever, just that simple.And the funny part was, I didn't even want to quit, nor was I concerned about smoking because I lived on cigarettes and coffee in construction. Not any more, and for that, I have thanked God many times, and it is a reminder, just how big of a thing it was for God to show me something special about that day, something that I will always carry with me. I never made that phone call to the man I met in the parking lot in that small town, and I also never held a grudge against that Super after that day.

I learned something else that day. I can go onto the next day without carrying any leftover hard feelings against people, even if they wronged me or tried to. It is something that has really helped me through some of the challenges I have had to go through. It has given me a cooler mind when dealing with those issues, so I can move forward with a clear head in order address some of those tough challenges, that, normally would eat you up inside. But there was much more learning ahead.

A number of years later, while traveling through California, we spent a day, my wife and I, in Carmel by the Sea, a small town near Pebble Beach Golf Course. We drove around and were awed by the waves, beaches, trees, birds and golf course, all intertwined, to create such breathtaking views. Later we ended up having lunch, on the sidewalk, in the artsy little town, followed by a walk through all the unique shops and galleries. As we came out of one store, John Travolta, walked out of the next one, and we met face to face, us in our summer casuals, him in a dark, broad shouldered, sports coat, and light slacks, with a male associate. I stopped right in front of him, and stuck out my hand, and exclaimed, "Why if it isn't John Travolta!", and immediately, his face lit up with a huge mouthed smile, he stuck out his hand, and gave us a "Its nice to meet you". I introduced ourselves, and, as he seemed to be enjoying the break in shopping, stood and chatted for a few minutes, then went on our ways. To this day, it has bothered me, that I didn't tell him, that there is a real GOD, he changed my life forever, and at the end of life's journey, if he is wrong by following some belief, made up by some man, as the scientology he believes in, he will end up in hell. I just want to tell him, as he is a smart person, gifted in many ways, to check it out better, I don't want him to miss out on heaven. I hope somehow, he will read this, and realize, the truth.

On the completion of that road project, I went back to the Head Office, and due to illness to the owner, ended up helping to ready all the equipment for selling at auction. It took months until auction day arrived, and by that time, a number of the supervisors, got together and decided, they would take up the owners offer of assisting to finance a company owned by them. In the end, two companies were formed. One owned by one group of supervisors that decided they wanted to go into building roads and subdivisions, and the other one, a group from the equipment side, that wanted to start a rental, repair, and trucking company, which I ended up in. I ran the equipment shop and crew, and eventually we got involved with a mine site operation in Alaska. So we sublet a mechanical crew into it, and started looking for, and trucking in equipment, to meet the demands of the new gold mine. I flew in every month and checked on the progress of our men and met with Mine Management for future needs. I had an opportunity, to observe, first hand, how the core samples and precious metal reports were produced to favor more investor interest. Something I would recall later in my life, when I traded my own stock portfolio. It went on for three years, and I got tired of flying and traveling, and I felt the need to do something on my own, so ended up leaving them to work in the direction of owning my own company. I had seen the advantage of the tax shelter offered by ownership, and up until then, I had made such a good living, I didn't mind paying the big income taxes. That was until the economy started changing, and with it, my thinking. I knew I had the ability to build and run my own business, and, along with that, I believed my work ethics and commitment, could prove success in anything I took on.

CHAPTER 5

Sometimes things happen that you have absolutely no control over, and how you handle it, can make a powerful impact on your understanding of life. Just like the time I was paralyzed from the waste down. I had decided to get into a business for myself, and an opportunity presented itself, so I worked hard to put a deal together. I met with the owner, of an auto repair shop, after hours, that was having financial troubles, and went through his business plan and after a number of meetings, showed him some different options of recovery. One included, was for me to run the business for him, on a salary, with a percentage of the profit, escalating every year with a buy-out option both ways. Another one, would have him institute some changes to the way he did business, by focusing on the profitable areas more and reducing the lower profit areas until his cash flow was better. Third, was a purchase by me with almost no goodwill, as the company had a bad reputation, and was going downhill fast. All three options would require of him, to get rid of his son that was basically running his business and stealing from it and lining his pocket with cash, faster than it could produce. After having time to decide which avenue to follow, he let me know he would continue on with my recommendations, and see what would happen, but with his son still employed. So my wife and I thought that was that, end of story, and I went on with my job, thinking that was most likely the last I would hear about it.

One year later, I got a call from the owner, to see if we could meet for coffee. I agreed thinking he was looking for further direction in his company, but it wasn't long after we met, that he asked me to buy the business from him. He had brought the Company's books with him, so I took a quick look, and on the spot, offered him $100,000. less than I had the year before. He was taken back a bit with the lower offer, so I pointed out where I saw that in his statements, and although he didn't want to understand that figure and maybe he didn't fully understand the numbers, he said he would think it over. We met once each week for three weeks, until we had a gentleman's sales agreement, subject to final finance approval. So off I went, to the Credit Union that I had dealt with for most of my life, with projections done with my brother, my accountant, and a business plan. They put the financing together, but had to wait until the next week for the Board to approve it. All was going ahead full speed, and we were set to take over the business, on the Tuesday morning following a holiday weekend. I had given notice to my employer and was at work on Thursday, my second last day, when I received a call from my wife, telling me to call the Credit Union representative, that had put the financing together. I called him, and he said he had made a mistake on the numbers that were approved, and now he would have to wait for another ten days for the board to meet again to approve the new finance schedule, and was concerned, that, the new numbers he had come up with, would not get approval. I was devastated. It was too late in the day to do anything, so when I got home that evening, my wife and I discussed the whole mess and then we decided we only had two choices. One was to wait for the Credit Union Board, but it didn't look positive, because the new figures meant we would have to come up with a lot more cash, which we didn't have. Option two, was to take all the files from the representative and take them to the bank that I had a personal account with for a number of years.We sat together and prayed, telling God, we had done everything we could to put this deal together but it didn't work, and we felt the door had slammed and if we were to get the business, He would have to intervene, otherwise we would accept it wasn't supposed to be.

In the morning, I called work to say I would be late, and went and picked up my folder full of my business plan and finances that were originally approved, and I took it to the bank. I asked to see a loans officer that could look at my business plan, and waited for the woman to find someone that could see me. Finally, she told me someone could see me later in the day and nobody was free at the moment. I urged her to convince someone just to give me five minutes with them, and relayed briefly what had transpired to get me here. With some convincing, she got me in to see a manager within half an hour. I walked in, introduced myself and spent all of the five minutes explaining what had happened, why and how, and this was all my paperwork and I had already quit my job, and was to take over the business in two days. I had written an approved cheque and now it was all halted. The manager, took my files, and promised me to go through them sometime today, and told me he would call me later that day during business hours for more information or with any direction of help he could offer. I left there, with a peace of mind, feeling I had done the best I could, to trust that whatever the outcome, was the way it was supposed to be. I just accepted it! Around 3:30 pm that Friday afternoon, I received a call from him, and all he said was " write the cheque from your account and come in next Tuesday and I will have all the paperwork done, just the way it was from the other guys. Congratulations, you just bought a business. Call me next week." WOW, the door just opened!! Wide open, and that is the way it would be.

The following Tuesday, I went in to our new business early, and put coffee on for the staff. When they came in, I introduced myself, as the new owner, their boss, and told them, starting immediately, they all just got a raise, because I didn't want anyone working for me that wasn't making a decent living. It would be up to them to prove, each of them deserved it, and, if they didn't live up to it, they would be gone. I promised that as long as they worked for me, I would ensure they would make a good pay cheque, but, if, number One they were dishonest, they were gone! Two, did not show pride in their work, and refused to change, gone! Third, I would set up training for them so they knew what to do in their jobs, if they did not learn, gone! Together we would make this business somewhere they would want all their friends and family to use. Those directions stayed in the forefront of our business, until the day we sold, twelve years later.

The business grew and grew, with lots of challenges in taking a company with a terrible record of customer abuse and dishonesty, to one that set the standard in the community for customer service and satisfaction, not to mention such dramatic increases in sales and profits. In the third year, out of the blue, I was asked if I would help put on a Christmas play at our church, and as I had never done anything like that, I said I would help. I thought I could probably help build some props or stairs or whatever, so I went to the meeting. As it turned out, the play turned out to be a major production, which would start in September to build the sets, and conclude in a week of evening productions the week before Christmas. And guess who would be in charge of the volunteers to build and also help produce the event, me. What did I get myself into? It was a major challenge to me, but it was a reward I would have never received if I wouldn't have taken the role. The production, was set in a winter village, that would have a choir and actors do a different play each year, that continued into the next year, for five years. The sets took thousands of man hours to build, and had to be made to take apart and reassemble each year, and still fit through doorways to storage rooms. It was probably one of the accomplishments of which I am most proud, for sticking it out. I met and worked with people from every walk of life, all volunteered, during the busiest time of the year, to tell the story of the true Christmas, to the people in the town they lived in. In the end, everyone that took part, got more out of it, and more out of Christmas than anyone else.

It was on a Thursday, in November in 1994, the third year of putting the Christmas production together when it happened. It was only two weeks away from opening night, and I was putting the final touches on the lighting and sound with those crews. The set was almost complete, and the first, practice pre-dress rehearsal was days away. It was less work now with the set familiar to us and well marked for assembly, and each group knew what would be required to make it work. I got up that normal morning, and went to the office to put on the coffee for the staff, for when they came in to start the day. Around 10:00 am, I ran an errand and when I got out of my pickup on returning to my business, I felt a sudden twinge in my lower back. I walked into my office and felt more discomfort as I sat at my desk, so I called my chiropractor and requested to come in as soon as possible for an adjustment. She told me she was booked for the day, but as she would normally accommodate me, she told me to come in on her lunch hour, and she would fit me in before her afternoon appointments. At noon I was at her office, and was told to take a chair and she would be back in fifteen to twenty minutes. I told the receptionist, I had to lift each leg into my truck to get here and had to take the elevator up to their office as I couldn't climb the stairs and I was afraid to sit down. She took me into one of the rooms and helped me lay down on the work bed, in considerable pain.

I lay there for a short time, when the chiropractor walked in very concerned of what she had been informed of my condition. I talked her through the events of the day and tried to help her understand my pain. She instructed me to sit up so she could check my back and I could not. She helped me, but the pain was so severe, I started sweating, groaning in pain, and holding my breath, and quickly she helped me lie back down. She tried to roll me over to no avail. She tried to gently pull my legs as to put traction on my spine, but the pain got worse. Over the next hour, everything just got worse, to the point I couldn't move my feet or legs, but when they were moved the pain was excruciating. It finally got to the point she had to call an ambulance. Two ambulance attendants, slide me onto their stretcher and took me to emergency at the hospital. My doctor, after a number of tests, with help, held me up with my feet touching the ground to try to help me stand, but my feet and legs would not have any part of it. He ran his pen hard down the bottom of my feet but I had absolutely no reflexes. He started me on morphine to try to ease the pain, which had continued to worsen as time went along. That night I was admitted to a hospital room as it seemed this was going in the wrong direction.

A few days went by, with blood tests, x-rays, and scans, and all the time on a continuous intravenous drip, with more and more morphine. I could not go to the bathroom since my arrival and my systems just started to shut down. Across from me in the room was a guy that just had surgery, and he told my wife that I must be in a lot of pain, because at night, under heavy drugs, I would cry out in pain all night long. My wife spent countless hours by my bed, and many of my friends would drop by, but I just lay there unable to move, but could talk to them in between dozing off from all the drugs. The fifth day in the room was really bad. The doctor had been in early that

Tuesday morning, and checked my reflexes and reports but was almost in disbelief at how I had deteriorated each day, to the point where he would pick up my leg, and just drop it back on the bed, without showing any muscle control or reflexes, but wincing in pain every time. A couple of my friend dropped by and prayed for me and told me they were missing me at the Christmas production, and they were all praying for my return. I thanked them and appreciated their commitment to taking time from their busy schedules, to stop by and visit me. I never ever thought about or prayed for my predicament. Maybe because of the drugs, I don't know. I was more concerned for everyone else and what I was putting them through. I didn't realize it until after it was all over.

My wife came in just before noon that day, and I was very drugged and not very responsive, which had her more concerned than normal. The drugs were filling up my body, and since I couldn't get rid of them by going to the bathroom, combined with the fact I couldn't take any liquids in, the level went up faster by the hour. A couple of hours after she got there, I blacked out! She screamed and the doctors and nurses came running!! The soon as they saw me, they knew what had happened, and the doctor started administrating a shot to get my heart pumping normal again, as it decided to shut down from the drug overdose in my system. When I came to, I was oblivious to what had happened, and as my mental state improved, she told me how scared I made her. She had tears in her eyes and the next few hours I could tell she really was scared, yet I didn't feel any emotions toward myself, only sorry I had put her through this. Finally, as if it had been on her mind for hours, felt it but didn't

JERRY TEMPLETON

know if or how to say it, but then said it in a way it cut through to the reality of the situation. Looking back, it must have been a desperate trust in faith, on both our parts, for what happened in the next few minutes. She got really close to me, held my hand, and while looking into my eyes, and almost right through me, and said "the doctors can't figure out what is wrong with you, and they don't know if you will be able to walk again, so it's up to you! IF you are going to walk, you are going to have to do it on your own"! I had never seen her so sure of what she had said, ever before. I looked at her, still coming from my drug overdosed state, and acting on what she believed, told her to get the walker, from the patient that used to be across the room, and put it beside my bed. Just as if she knew the end of the story, she wasted no time in positioning it beside me, and tried her best, to partly sit me up, with me trying to carry myself on my arms and swing my legs over the edge of the bed. Since the previous Thursday morning, I had been unable to sit at all and to allow my legs to hang over the edge was impossible, unless two people held me up so there was no pressure on my spine. Somehow we managed, me on my arms, her helping best she could, working together, to get in that position. And she looked at me, with a determination for me, and said,"the rest is up to you". Something happened that moment, that didn't register until a few minutes later, and that is the part, that just is beyond understanding, myself. I walked the twelve steps to the bathroom and closed the door, and sat on the toilet. And, that is the first moment, I knew, without a doubt!!

The moment I sat down, it hit me, and tears started streaming down my face, uncontrolled. I just realize, I had actually carried the walker across the room, without a twinge of pain, from the moment both feet had hit the floor. One second before, the pain was as strong as it ever was, but that step of faith, completely restored my muscles, my spine and released the pain completely from my body. The shock and realization, came out of me in the form of tears, lots of happy tears, and I just sat there for a good five minutes, and urinating, the first time in six days. As I opened the door and stepped out into the room, I walked past my wife to my bed and sat down! I wish I had a picture of the look on my wife's face. Yes, she had tears, and there was a flushed look, but there was also a sort of glow, of understanding, of what had just happened, before I spoke. As I cried through my effort to explain, I told her I had been healed, completely, almost as if I never knew how bad the pain had been, and not only my body, but my whole being!! We had just got our emotions under control, and I was still sitting on the edge of my bed, my wife sitting in the chair a few feet away, when around the corner into my room walked my brother. He took two steps in, stopped, and with a shocked expression on his face, turned and left without so much as saying one word. About three minute later, giving himself time to get over the shock, he re-entered the room, walked half way to my bed and asked what in the world was going on. He knew the odds of my walking again were slim or worse, but to see the change, from the day before, was totally unexpected, and unbelievable. I stood up as if to prove the changes, even to myself again, and felt as if I had never laid there for almost a week. I threw on a robe, and we walked the hallways as if I had a brand new body, without any stability problems or muscle pains, and without any assistance from anyone. WOW!!! The nurses came and explained, they were concerned for my safety because normally anyone that has had any paralysis for any length of time, will have problems with strength and control of their legs, and reminded me that just this same morning my body had shut down, because of a drug overdose. They also reminded me I had nothing to eat or drink for six days and could pass out with out warning. I just kept walking and feeling something special, and didn't ever want to forget that moment or that newness feeling I had.

Later that evening, the doctor came through the door, relaying, what he had heard from the nurses, about the changes to me. He had me stand beside the bed, and lean on it with both hands, and as if to break me of this healing I told him about, he took his fist, and hit me up and down my spine, about eight times, hard enough to injure a healthy person. I just laughed, and reminded him I was healed, and there was nothing he could do other than accept it. We sat down in the chairs beside my bed, and he explained, he had done all the tests possible, except one that had to be done in the city, and he had set that nuclear medicine test up for the next day. He requested I stay in the hospital, one more day, and be taken by ambulance in for testing and back the same day, as he had gone to great lengths to set it up, and, if there was something wrong in me, this would show it. I agreed with him, reminding him they would find absolutely nothing, because, I was completely healed, without a doubt.

The next morning, as per schedule, I was whisked away for the tests. As they set me up and injected me for the tests, I answered all the questions concerning what had taken place as written in the file that had accompanied me there. The nurse monitoring me throughout the procedure, explained, that most people she saw, that had encountered what I had gone through, never recovered fully and many, never walked again. She said that, she believed in miracles and from what she read in my file, she had no doubt, I had received one. During the tests, I lay motionless, on a cold tray of a bed, and a scanner moved across me and would stop every few inches, and I could watch on the computer screen, as parts of my spine, each separately, rotated 360 degrees as different parts were measured and checked by the computer. It was amazing to watch your own body parts. At the end, the technician said, if she hadn't read my reports, she would have never though anything had ever happened to me, because, there was nothing visible to her from the tests. She explained, even if something had been wrong and was rehabilitated, there would be telltale signs of the injury site. She said, due to the circumstances of my report, she spent more time examining the process to try to find anything at all, pointing to a damaged area, but found nothing. I thanked her for doing her best, and concluded my visit by informing her, that, anything God fixed, would be fixed just like brand new. They took me back to my hospital, sitting up, and as soon as I got back, I was checked out and went home, changed forever, inside and out. Thank-you God! Many others deserved it more!

CHAPTER 6

I came from a family, with one older sister, then me, next, a younger sister, then brother, then baby sister. Five kids, a mom and dad, and never too much extra for our parents to raise us with. We did fine, learned some lessons on values. Dad volunteered for the Fire Department, and Civil Defense. The Civil Defense was set up to oversee emergency response, originally for post wartime and then for any emergency. Once a year, they would have to sort through their inventory, and sell off, the dated, stored goods, cheap. They would dump the water but they would sell cases of Prem, the canned meat, cheap! You know, the stuff with jelly around it. Of course, we ended up buying cases of it, so, mother, would concoct one hundred different ways to prepare it, or should I say disguise it, but you always knew what it was. We had some pretty good memories to hold onto. Roast beef dinners on Sunday, after church, even though many years the beef was moose, deer, elk, pheasant or pork, it still was special. Mom was of English descent, and she always had at least two deserts to choose from, even if one was made out of rice and milk, and the other was from something we grew in our garden. Dad worked many years as a truck driver and sometimes would be gone on trips for a week or so. Mom always did holidays up special, and would always invite company over to share the day with.

She made sure we were raised in the church, and she played the piano and the organ during the services, self taught. She made sure we had good values for life, about God and about people and how to do the best for both. I know many times when I was young, dad got into tough places with his finances. He always had trouble showing any emotions other that mad. When I was about twelve years old, I heard mom and dad arguing after all of us kids went to bed. Something had been bothering him for a number of days, and he didn't say anything to anyone, he would just hold everything in, and just fume, until something would give. I felt the "give" a few times in my growing up, until the day I was old enough to stand up to him. Don't get me wrong, I loved and respected him, but there was also a serious fear factor involved. Anyway, this night he was heated, and blew, and I was down in my bedroom in the basement, and heard all the words coming out of his rage. I was only twelve. After a few hours, I heard him threaten mom, saying he was going to shoot her and then himself, and he was convincing, mom was pleading, I was crying and petrified. I didn't know what to do, but I knew he had a pistol from the Air Force, and I knew his rages. Out of shear panic, I climbed out the bedroom window, without a coat, and ran through the pouring rain, to the pastors house, about two miles away, crying all the way, not knowing what was happening or what I would find when I got back. The Pastor, listened to my plea through tears of concern and fright, then wisely called my home, and explained I was there, and my state of concern, and asked if they needed someone to talk to. He went over and I spent the night at his house with his son and family, and whatever went on that night, ended in some kind of resolve, as, when I returned the next day, nothing was said until a day later. Mom, came to me and said she was sorry I had been so upset.

Dad bought a garage repair shop, with a partner, when I was a teenager, so I worked for him after school and on Saturdays, pumping gas, washing vehicles, cleaning up and even learning to work on vehicles. I did grease jobs, oil changes, tire repairs, and helped the mechanics. He paid me $2.00 per week, and I always thought I was getting ripped of, but that was the way it was. He was on the volunteer fire department, so when I turned fourteen, I was allowed to be on it too. I grew with the volunteer department for over twenty years. After I was married, I ended up as a training officer for the firemen, and also for the "rescue Squad," that was started in order to rescue people trapped in auto accidents, and ended up for every kind of help required in our area. Eight men, took training to the same qualifications as that of the Ambulance Attendants, and some of them ended up working as Ambulance Attendants or Firemen for the rest of their careers. We saw things most people should never have to see. Lots of memories, some good, some sickening, some just plain awful.

One Thanksgiving day, I was just sitting down to turkey dinner, when, my pager went off, and I took off in response. We ended up in a well to do neighborhood, where a man had cut a tree down about one hundred yards from his house, and when we arrived, we found a wife and two young children, on the back porch, with very shocked expressions on their faces, pointing to the back ravine area. We found her husband, their dad, laying on the ground, on his side, with his chest and the side of his head, caved in, gurgling in his fluids, with no hope of surviving. We could have just called a coroner, but because the family was nearby, but not in view, we decided to load him and transport him, to allow us to remove him from his home with the least bit of extra stress on his young family. It would have been his choice, if he was given it, but he died, before we left the driveway. After returning home, a few hours later, almost sick to my stomach, and thinking of that young family and their Thanksgiving day, I sat down to eat my dinner that was saved for me, and, not wanting to ruin my family's day, choked down the food. Later, when I explained the day to my wife, it was all I could do, to keep from crying, but, that is why we did such a good job as a squad. We took everything to heart, as if every patient was our family.

One day, we responded to an attempted suicide. We had to walk through a swamp for about one half of a mile, over fences, through water filled ditches, with a basket, to bring out a twenty-one year old young man, that had shot himself through the head, with a twenty-two calibre rifle, and was still alive. When we got to him, guided by a young police officer that had already found him, he was laying on the wet ground, with a hole through his head, that you could put your small finger through, about one inch in front of his ear. He was convulsing, and still breathing, and the bullet had ruined his brain, but he had not bled much so his heart was still going strong. We loaded him in the basket, and took almost an hour getting him back out because our feet would sink in the swamp with the extra weight. When we finally finished, we lay exhausted on the roadside, in silence, absolutely wasted, as we each went through the chain of events, in our minds.

Another rainy night, we arrived on a scene, with one car upside down, in the middle of the road, with gas running down onto the trapped occupants. The other car, was almost totally unrecognizable, 100 yards away with a seriously injured driver. We had rescued both unconscious, injured people from the front seat of the upside down, crushed car, while the firemen hosed us down the whole time. When we thought we had finished, someone heard a faint baby cry from the back seat of the car. I slid my hand up between the twisted metal, and sure enough, I could feel a baby car seat, hanging upside down, with gasoline running down it. We sprang into operation, with an urgency only a parent could understand. And most of us had young children. No one could see the child, and no one could get two hands in there at once, so off came our protective gear, on came the fire hoses, and while one hand of one man held the baby up into the car seat, someone else's hand, with a special cutter in it, whittled away at the nylon straps. It took some time and the rescuers had to take turns, due to the awkward position and difficulty in working invisibility, and not wanting to cut the baby. Finally, free from its tomb, the baby slid down the arms, unscathed, to safety, soaked in gasoline, but alive. Rewarding, is not a word that could come close.

We risked being seriously or even critically burned for that child, but, if we had to do it again, we wouldn't even hesitate for a second. Some days, one of us would have to go around the side of the rescue vehicle and throw up, in the middle of a job, then return like nothing happened, and continue working. After every call, on returning to the hall, we would sit down, and discuss what had happened, the good, the bad, or what could have helped, and how everyone was, and that was that.

Between volunteer fireman, playing baseball through the summer, camping, fishing on weekends with the family, and working overtime, I was just blessed with more energy than most. We were married in 1970, and had our first absolutely perfect daughter, in February 24,1972. I rushed my wife into the hospital at 11:00pm on a Tuesday night, nineteen months later, October 11,1973, and sat in the waiting room for our next child. There was a lot of commotion that night, as I watched anxiously from the end of the hall, for a nurse to come and tell me what we had. At around 2:00 am, a nurse came down the long hallway, and asked me my name. On telling her, she said "Congratulations, you can come and see your daughters now"! I replied, confused by her mistake," DAUGHTERS'?? to which she replied, "didn't anyone tell you, you have twin daughters, born at 12:30 and 12:35"!,

"TWINS"? I almost yelled in a high pitch. "YES! TWINS!, and they are doing just fine"! She took me to my wife, that had just come out of surgery to remove the placenta, that was destroyed but would not release from her. She was groggy and drained, but looked up at me and asked if she did a good job, then the nurses brought the girls out so we could touch them for a moment. Shocked! Thrilled! Surprised! Scared! Broke? NO, BLESSED!! We had the three best things we could ever have imagined possible. Three daughters that grew up to be our best friends. Which brought us three of the greatest sons (in laws to most) and would lead to nine grand children, for which we are blessed every day to the end of our lives. Family... Our very own!

A number of years later, I got a phone call while on summer holidays with our kids. It was from my mother, and she never called, so I knew it wasn't a good call. She told me, she was sorry for having to call and didn't want to ruin my holiday with my family, but wanted to tell me herself. We had a very good relationship, and in some ways, we shared some of the same emotions. She told me just found out she had cancer, and the doctors couldn't do anything for her, and she only had a couple of months to live! I would say, that changed me big time!! Not long after that, she died. I would have a different outlook on life. I explained it simply, "like looking through different eyes"! I saw many things in a different light, so to speak. People, and how they were doing, was more important. "Things", lost their value, and "taking time," replaced it. Why losing a mother could have such an effect on my whole family, much more that losing our father, which happened twenty-six months later? He counted the days on his calendar, starting when she died, for the next two years, then just quit counting. Two months later, he went to Palm Springs, California, and the following week, I got a telephone call, from his friends he was with, and the voice on the other end, just said,"your dad's gone, he died about half an hour ago, there was nothing they could do for him"! Just like that... They had gone out for supper, got back to where they were staying, changed and went to the pool for an pre-bedtime swim. Dad went to the pool bathroom, saying he ate too much chicken, and his stomach was upset, and when he never came back out, his best friend went in and found his laying in one of the stalls, dead! Massive coronary, the coroner said. Both parents had passed away in their 66th year.

Did you ever notice, bad things usually happen in groups of three's? We always remarked about it in the fire department and the ambulance service, but it seems to be common in every day life. I can remember one of those worst case, three's, I had to deal with, that would take a few years out of my life. One Tuesday morning around 11:00, I got a call from my best friend's wife, quite distraught. She said, Larry, her husband, was in the next town, at a specialist's office. They found he had brain tumor, and she wanted me to drive her there, so she could drive him home in his truck, as the doctor said he couldn't drive. Shock number one! The same week, we were told my wife's brother, had prostate cancer, and they were going to have to operate immediately to stop it from spreading. Number two!! A couple of days later, even worse!! My baby sister, in her 41st year, was diagnosed with a cancerous tumor, in her kidney, and she would end up dying, within a few months. Number three!!! And that one, our family never has recovered from completely.

After my dad died, I was numbed a bit. I remember going to work, the week following his funeral, and only half a mile from home, I was pulled over by an officer of the law, for speeding. I didn't even care. He walked up to the window of my vehicle, and asked if I knew that I was speeding, and I replied, I could have been. He took my license and insurance and went to his car to write a ticket. When he came back, he looked at me for a second, then asked if I was OK, and I informed him I was not, due to the fact my dad had just passed away the week before, and I was still a bit in shock. He took another look at my license, and, as if a light bulb came on in his head, he asked "was Ernie, your father?", and without waiting for an answer, he rambled thoughts after thoughts,"I knew him, he was great guy, he helped me out a couple of times, sorry he passed away, you got enough on your mind, you don't need this so I'll take care of it, drive carefully". And with that, he tore up the ticket and walked back to his car, leaving me to sit there with a few tears in my eyes. That was probably the nicest thing my dad ever did for me! For the next months, I just worked and didn't really want to do anything fun, until one weekend, my wife talked me into going away to this resort with a group from the church, that were going hiking, swimming golfing, etc, just for a get-a-way. I wasn't really interested and when she said to throw my golf clubs in the trunk, I just didn't feel like it. At the last minute, I threw them in just in case.

I ended up going golfing, to complete the foursomes, as someone couldn't make it. I met this Larry guy, and from the moment we met, something just clicked and over the next years, became best of friends. It started out as golfing buddies, but as both of us were businessmen, it progressed to a special relationship. Most men, never have someone in their life like we had with each other, and most men need a friend like that, even just once. But not a day went by, without Larry and I going for coffee or lunch, or talking on cell phones, from where ever in the world, either of us would be, or traveling somewhere together. We shared all our thoughts with each other, personal, business, life in general, and never ever, repeated any of it to anyone else, and, also, never held anything said, against each other. It was great to have someone, that I could say exactly what was on my mind to, without any judgment, just to get it off my chest, sometimes not too nice and sometimes serious thoughts, which I had thought, I was the only one in the world, that thought things like that. We laughed together a lot, and many times at each other.

Then that day came, with the call from his wife. When he ended up in surgery a week later, the Surgeons, had to cut his head from ear to ear, right over the top, and removed a small orange sized tumor, from his left temple. I drove the one hour in to the hospital to see him every day following the surgery, and sometimes twice the same day, until he was allowed to go home. The next morning, after his surgery, he couldn't talk and didn't seem to recognize his wife and daughters, but when I walked in and said "Hi Larry", his eyes lit up, and I knew he remembered me. He had to learn to walk, talk, and all the normal things for real life, and eventually, he learned how to golf again. A year following his surgery and radiation treatments, we got to cruise to Alaska, travel with our wives on a golf trip to Murtle Beach, and a few more holidays, before he started to deteriorate. His life end, a couple of years after his first diagnosis. One of the toughest duties I have had in my life up to that time, was to stand at his celebration of life, and tell the gathering about my best friend. This was what I said;-

"I would like to tell you about my friend. To many people, he was quiet and listened a lot, but didn't say too much. When he spoke you could tell he had thought it over first, and I never saw him lose his temper, ever. He was always positive, well, almost always. He loved to golf, and, one day, we were golfing and had to tee off across a lake to an island green. He hit his ball and it landed twenty yards short, in the water. We had each just purchased a new box of balls, so, he casually walked over, took another ball, and hit it, twenty yards short, again. After about his eighth ball, I said to him he should try a different iron, but he sort of mumbled that he just didn't get all of it, so I watched, until he teed up the last ball from his box. I reminded him of the distance, and breeze, and chuckled out loud reminding him, this was his last ball. He stopped, looked at me, nodded and laughed, "then you better hope I make it, you still have eleven balls I can use", and with that, he put his shot on the green. He sat back down in the cart as if nothing had happened, looked at me, and said "and you thought I couldn't do it" and then laughed.

He loved to laugh, but not at others expense. And we laughed a lot, sometimes more like two school kids, usually at each other. One time I was in a sand trap, and I miss-hit the ball and it flew across the green, hit a tree, landed and rolled back across the green, stopping about 6 inches from dropping in the lake. I felt pretty lucky, and as I walked out of the trap, proud of my "great" shot, I looked over to see him kick it into the lake. He looked up at me with a long and serious look and piped "You weren't going to take that were you?" and with that, his big hearty laugh. What could you do, but laugh. He loved sports, never gave up on the Vancouver Canucks, hockey team, just enjoyed them as they were, entertainment. He loved movies, loved traveling. One of us would say something like "wouldn't it be nice to go,..wherever?" and the next day, I would get a call with flight times and dates, with about 10 minutes extra, to make it to our first tee time, already booked. I guess that's how sometimes he got nicknamed "Maserati". I don't think we were ever late if he drove, and he loved to drive! If you were to meet somewhere, you could set your watch by him, and sometimes we would! He loved to read, but I think reading bored him, because, usually when he sat down to read, he would fall asleep,,a power nap,, fifteen minutes, and then, as quick,"LETS GO" where ever, maybe for desert, maybe not!

He cared about and helped people, sometimes total strangers. He was very giving, especially if he felt someone was down or maybe just not fortunate in life. And, he didn't want to take any credit for helping others in need. He told me he was very fortunate to be able to help, and it was sort of a rule, "IF YOU COULD, YOU DID"!

We traveled and enjoyed each others company. We called each other from no matter where our travels took us. From Alaska to Murtle Beach, and anywhere in between, we did it up right! One day he said to me, the toughest thing he ever had to do, was to stay positive through his months of surgery recovery. Today, he's in heaven with Payne Stewart, and a few others he wanted to meet, and someday, I will hear him laugh again. Did I mention? My friend's name is Larry!"

My brother in law, went through his surgery good, and we have spent many days traveling, golfing and making some great memories. My sister, on the other hand, had never been sick in her life, and suddenly developed back pain, so immediately went to see her doctor, who referred her directly, to an x-ray technician. Right from that x-ray, there was a concern for her life. Before she could have exploratory surgery, she would have to have a number of blood transfusions, and originally we were told there was a tumor in one of her kidneys, but when they finally did operate, the tumor had attached to a major blood vessel and had grown to the size of a small watermelon, reducing the kidney to minuscule dimensions, the size of a kidney bean. They removed the tumor and said there was nothing else they could do. It was a couple of months before she died. She knew she was going to die, and asked if we would all pray, that she would not have pain, as that was the only thing she was afraid of. Our prayers were answered. All of her family visited her so she was never left alone, and shortly before her last day, when I was alone with her, I asked her how it really was. She said it was awful! Not the part about dying, but the part about watching everyone come and go, and everyone trying their best to put on a good front. She could tell all the time, they were feeling sick on the inside, but none could put it into words. No one wanted to make her feel any worse than they thought she did, and she didn't want them to feel any worse than they did. Laying on her death bed, she was the one that made everyone laugh at her comic attitude towards the hospital life, and especially the food or jello. She died, months before her 41st birthday, and took with her, a part of all of us, and more of some of us. What a shame it was to loose the spark plug of our family, but I was glad that, mom and dad, had both died before her, so they wouldn't have to witness the end of her life.

We still miss you Shirl!

CHAPTER 7

"10 OUT OF 10 DIE!" That is what I read one day on a bumper sticker, and I just couldn't get it out of my head. There must be millions of things people feel they need to say, on cars, shirts, hats, billboards, TV, the list is endless, and most of the time, you react in some way. You usually repeat what you read to someone, because they are funny or stupid, and sometimes, they cause you to stop and have a feeling about what shock value was produced, or who would wear such a statement? But most of the time, you forget what you saw or read, usually sooner than you can regurgitate it for someone else. Not this one!..it's so true. DIE?? WE ALL WILL!!

When our daughters were teenagers, we went by van to Disneyland in California for a quick trip. Before we headed back to Canada, we went to visit my cousin that lived within thirty minute of where we were staying. Her grandmother, my Aunt, had been visiting her for a month and was planning to head back to Sacramento, about a nine hour drive. As we were going right by there, we invited her along for the ride. She was in her early eighties, and lived with her daughter since her husband passed away. He had been an Preacher and Evangelist, that traveled all over the world, preaching the gospel, in tent meetings. We talked for hours, it went by too quickly and it was a great memory!

She told of their trip to London, England, in the 1960's, for Harold to preach in a week of tent meetings held there. She said, it wasn't long after they got to London, that she came down with some kind of sickness, and within a few days, ended up in the hospital, and then went into a coma. Every day following his preaching, he would come and pray for her and sit by her, never fully understanding the severity of her illness, just trusting she would be okay. During the beginning of the last tent meeting, the doctor sent a messenger to let Harold know, his wife was on the edge of death and he should come at once. He got the message, but felt he needed to conclude the crusade, and she was going to be fine, or so he thought. Before he got to the hospital later that day, my Aunt was pronounced dead! The doctor and nurse, covered her body with a sheet, filled out the paperwork, and waited for her husband to return.

My Aunt continued to share this experience, as we drove. She said, she was unaware of anything in regards to the doctor or nurses as they tried to keep her alive. She did recall, she saw a brightness, like the sun, bright, warm, but you could look into it, and she got closer and closer, ever so slowly, and then, she was surrounded by a "liquid love", submersed in it!! It was the best thing you could ever want and she did not want to leave it. She could not say how long she was in this liquid love, but she felt she was slowly being drawn out of it and away from it, and although there were no words, she expressed from her heart she did not want to leave it. In the next instant, she was awake, and sat up in bed, just moments after Harold walked into her room, and just after he was told she had passed away, gone! As she sat up, and the sheets dropped from her face and body, she said, "HAROLD! I'M READY TO GO"! And with that, if front of the shocked doctor and nurse, while they tried to check her vital signs, she dressed and they left. Harold told her after, he believed she was going to recover, he felt it from God, and felt at peace, knowing she was in God's hands!!! That day with us, she told it just like she lived it, those many years earlier, and in a peaceful, gentle tone, never having to stop to recall the events. I have thought of that liquid love many times since then!

My wife and I were enjoying the sun in Palm Springs, California, when I got an e-mail from one of my daughters, which included a video she was sent, via a friend, that showed a Pastor, that had been going through the process of losing his voice, with the Doctors, unable to prevent it. He was speaking, at a convention, with great difficulty, with a voice that was squeaking and crackling, and at times he would have to pause, for a moment, to try to gather enough wind, to force his voice to complete the sentence. Anyway, as he was trying his best, out of the blue, without at first him even noticing it, his voice got clearer and clearer, with less and less effort, until suddenly, he noticed what was happening, and, right in the middle of his sentence, he stopped, and with a tearful but totally submissive, thankful, prayer like voice, stated,

GOD was healing him, right then, right in that moment. He thanked GOD for allowing him to talk again, and continued his speaking, stopping now and again, to praise GOD for what he was going through. Not just for the healing, but for allowing him to have that feeling, that a power greater than anything known to mankind, was surging through him, leaving no doubt in his mind, his body was touched and was changing. WOW!

As I had just seen that 10 out of 10 bumper sticker, a few days earlier, I replied back to her the following;-

"It is another sunny and warm day (boring you may think) not boring when you wear shorts, golf, barbecue salmon for dinner, you know, and so on and so on. But you know what, we still miss you and all the day to day things that go on. Thanks for sending that "voice healing story", impressive. Mom and I, wonder, what you think or recall, of the total healing/miracle, I had, when I was paralyzed in the hospital, and they overdosed me, almost stopped my heart, and almost lost me. How I never ever prayed for my own healing, only for those around me, that they would not worry, and when, as they drugged me more and more, how I accepted being paralyzed and the Doctors tested me and basically said, they could do nothing but drug me to kill the pain, but they couldn't even stop the pain. Don't know if you all know the whole story, of how mom played an important part in, giving me the motivation, to take my first, and what proved to be, the ONLY step, I needed, to be healed. I will never forget, the emotions I went through, and have told my story, to many non believers and Christians alike, and it still brings me to tears, even when I write this to you. The power or the healing of GOD, is so indescribable, that you are left, just wondering, "why me?", so undeserving, so far down the list of people that need healing worse, but leaving me feeling, that there must be something bigger ahead. In a bigger picture, that I could not understand if I did know. That is the power of prayer for others, without looking for any credit, but at the same time, accepting those things, you can't change, but not letting them discourage you. I will never understand, why my youngest sister, Shirley died, but I know, she was special to me and others, and I just try to be thankful, for knowing her the way I did, and the special place she had in MY life! We saw a bumper sticker this week, that said it all, something to remember...."10 OUT OF 10 DIE"...his other sticker, said something about JESUS, but the 10 thing stuck, how true! We all fit in the 10 out of 10, we just do not know when and we are not supposed to live our lives worrying about WHEN, we are only to concern ourselves with HOW we spend our time, while we are here, making a difference, or not. Love you all, can't wait to see you all, have a good week, love mom and dad."

Her reply;-

> "I like that bumper sticker,"10 out of 10 die"..that's a good thing to remember when life gets overly busy and I need to refocus!
>
> I remember when you were paralyzed. I remember hating Dr. Janzen even more than ever. I remember when you walked those few steps from your bed to the chair and it was so overwhelmingly

awesome and precious and miraculous.
Shawn and I talk of it every once and
awhile...were we engaged then?! I
think so.

Are you coming home for Easter?"

All three of our daughters were married within the
previous twelve months of my paralysis/healing episode,
including this one, that was wed three weeks prior. It
is interesting, how such a miraculous, unprecedented,
unreal, life changing event can happen, yet within my
family, I never took the time to ensure, every detail, every
feeling, every thought that occurred, was relayed to our
kids, so somehow they could be as close as possible to
that feeling I had experienced. Oh don't get me wrong, I
told everyone I came into contact with about my experience, but I must have felt, my family were caught up in it,
and knew everything about it. So in the busyness of our
lives at that time, I took it for granted, that my kids knew
my true feelings and thoughts. Missed the boat that time!
Good lesson! If my kids are so important, I had better
make sure they know how I really feel, about the things I
have experienced, both good and bad, so they understand
everything that goes into the make up of their parent.

A year later, our first grandchild was born, a girl, not
just any girl, our very first, only ever first, but she was ours,
and was she special. When the first one of our daughters
decided to get married, and after our son in law to be,
asked me for her hand, her mom and I cried, a mixture
of emotions, all the wishes you carry for you child, all
the unknowns that lie ahead for them, all the excitement

in having their own everything, including fulfilling your dreams of getting grandchildren, all rolled into one. That new little granddaughter didn't let us down, one bit. She was beautiful, perfect in every way, and the moment we set eyes on her, knew she was our precious little gift, from GOD. We cried tears of joy over her, we were so excited. That was October 30! THREE months later, we were gathered in a different hospital room, with our now lifeless, little angel, within hours from possibly the end of her life. She had somehow, contracted, a viral infection, which was attacking her blood cells. They had taken so many blood samples, they told us they couldn't take any more until 6 am the next morning, to determine, if they would give her a blood transfusion, that might help her live. Nothing had helped so far, and the last blood sample was insufficient, due to the lack of blood in her body, to give adequate testing. They had to milk the blood from her! She had her young mom and dad, and her grandparents, that, never left her alone, for even a moment in the hospital, and although there was nothing they could do but cradle the motionless, tiny, precious, bundle, they never gave up, but trusted and prayed to GOD, to intervene, in making her body well again. That night was long and sleepless, and in the morning, the report from the tests, showed, a very tiny amount of improvement in her blood count. An ever so slight sign, that our prayers had not been in vain. She was not better, but, there was a sign, not to give up praying and trusting, that she would recover. Over the next few hours, then days, then weeks, she was returned to all of us, to continue her life, and to allow us all of those dreams we carried, for her and her life. Life is so precious but oh so fragile. Nineteen years later, this little angel God allowed us to keep, gave us our first great granddaughter. And after she recovered from her close call, we were blessed with eight more grandchildren, nine in all, five boys, and four girls, all just as precious.

Years later, my wife and I were at a funeral of friend, and when we went in, I put my cell phone on "quiet" but "vibrate". Halfway through the service, my phone started vibrating, and I just reached down and stopped the vibration, and waited until after to answer it. Later that day, in conversation, I compared the end of life, to a cell phone call. There you are sitting, minding your own business, when, suddenly without warning, irregardless of what or where you are, your cell phone rings. Instead of the phone ringing, it could be the end of your life calling, heart attack, accident, gunshot, anything, just like that, THE END!!!!! That is just how close we are at any given time! No one is exempt, no one has a "get out of jail free" card in life, no one knows, just when that call will come. No matter if you are rich or poor, sickly or seemingly healthy, the call comes, your gone, its over, final!! And yet, we are not to spend time worrying about it, or that too, could shorten your life. We are told by our friends, enjoy life to the fullest, our parents, give everything you do, 100%, and wear clean underwear, and from our pastors, to make a difference in someones life, for the better, and, love one another. They are all right, but if we look around, it seems, most of us, are in the collecting,"the guy with the most toys wins", mode. And, the more money you seem to have, the more toys you accumulate, or so it seems.

But wait! I have a secret, I want to share with everyone. I always say, "it all averages out in the end", meaning, you make money on some things, loose on others, but in big picture, it usually works out to the good. But there is more! For years, I went to church, especially on special occasions, Christmas, Easter, you know, and I worked hard, made a great living, bought everything we needed and more, and still managed to save, and get ahead. At least until I was around thirty-six years old. Had money in the bank, sometimes, quite a bit! I had done pretty good! Pretty good, why bother, when there is so much more available. I learned it by accident, although, I had been told many times, just how it worked, I guess I didn't believe it or, I did so good on my own, that I didn't need any help. Did I miss out!

I started to tithe, give ten percent of my income to the church and special charities, but more important, back to GOD! I was aware of any monies I gave back, of how it was used. That is called stewardship, not just the giving, but the followup, to make sure your giving was used properly. I gave of my income and my time. There probably are hundreds of books written, on tithes and offerings, and giving, but this is not one of them. You will know, if you really believe, you are giving back that which is not yours to keep. Anyway, the more I gave, the more I ended up with. Then the cycle would just keep improving. Not always like you think. All different ways. Deals would just happen, things would come along that would just give you better returns than you thought possible. And, along with, more and more, comes friends you end up meeting, that give even more, and you end up, not only rewarded with some awesome friendships, but stories they share of how they have been given back, over and over, only to have so much more. It is the one of the best things you can do in life. If you have never heard it before, listen closely, YOU CAN NEVER OUTGIVE GOD!!!!! There it is, it's true, it's factual, it really is. Give, not to get back, but because it is not yours to keep, and, God will reward you for being a good steward of his money, and just keeps on giving, knowing you will give even more. Another lesson, so simple, yet so rewarding, and so fulfilling.

We never tried to sell our auto repair business, because it had turned successful, but when someone came along, and asked what we wanted for it, we both felt, as long as they met the concerns we had, for the future for the staff and customers, we were supposed to sell it. We had a problem with one of our main employee's a few years earlier, and it seemed there would always be a concern regarding his honesty. He had stolen money from the Company on a number of occasions, and I always felt, no one else would give him a second chance, but I would. I would put more safeguards in place every time, and he would be good for a while but would always push me to the the maximum, even though he was getting paid extremely well, with achievable bonuses in place, for him to make even more. When he stole the last time, I was told by the police and by the Labor Relations Office, to charge him and throw him in jail, because, he would just end up continuing his stealing down that road, with his next employer. I felt it would have a negative effect on his young family, and as he had four children, I would rather take the chance of making an honest person out of him. Although it caused many restless nights, I still believe I made the right decision, and after all was said and done, it all averaged out, the business sold. Even better, we were good stewards and took care of our staff, were involved in improving peoples lives, and helped many organizations and churches, and in the end, sold at the top of the market, without trying to sell, for exactly what we thought the company was worth. GOD had a part in all of it!

Shortly before the offer came to purchase our business, an opportunity came, for me to return to Grenada, in the West Indies, to help rebuild after a tornado disaster in 2004. I stated I would like to be a part of the team being assembled from British Columbia and Alberta, Canada, and if it didn't work for me to go, I would support the group financially. The business sold, I got all my shots, and six weeks later, I was off to help, however, doing whatever, wherever, in Grenada. Conditions were pretty grim on arrival, and a group of twenty of us, were ushered, in the sweltering heat, to mosquito infested, dorm type buildings, with an outdoor cooking and eating area. We had brought some food with us, and had collected money from all, to buy additional food supplies as required. We had limited refrigerator space, and had two from our group, responsible for feeding us, ride to town daily to find whatever food they could, to maintain our health. Due to the disaster, everything was limited, and what supplies were available, had a significant price attached to them. That went for everything, from food, to building supplies. As it was a third world country, transportation, was limited, not only from the poor roads and damage from the storm, but compounded by the demand for gas and diesel fuel, by all of the outside agencies, there to help rebuild the island. It had been destroyed! The massive rain forests were gone, half the buildings were destroyed, or severely damaged. All you saw, no matter where you went, were blue tarps, covering almost every roof, that had been torn off. The steel "I" beam soccer stadium, was all twisted in an unrecognizable pile. What used to be the field, was now a dumping area, a mountain of discarded roofing steel and aluminum, all twisted and torn. The beaches were gone, the palm trees, just shredded posts, or nothing at all. You just stood in amazement, that anyone survived at all, and yet, we understood, only a few perished.

From our sleeping and eating headquarters, we would be driven daily, about 45 minutes, to an area, that once had a church in the middle of thousands of trees, many that produced the spices the island is renown for, and surrounded by small houses, or to us, shanty's. Many, only having one lite bulb, and most, not having running water. Everyone would share an outside, hand pump for water, that would be witness to morning personal bathing's. As communication was months away from returning to the area, due to devastation of the power lines and telephone wires, we strung an extension cords for hundreds of yards, from a plugin, in a one room, house/store, that was fortunate to be on the end of a power line. Although, some days the power was off, it did help us considerably, and we paid the old woman in the store daily for using it. Most residents in the area, walked anywhere they were going, which wasn't far, and every morning, we watched the men, dressed in tattered clothing, with machete's over their shoulders, heading out to clear the fallen jungles, by hand, so they could replant new spice groves. Before the hurricane, from the buildings we were working on, you could only see trees and the hot sun, beating straight

JERRY TEMPLETON

down on you, but now, we enjoyed a 240 degree view of the ocean, along with the suns burning rays.

We were going to rebuild a church and a house beside it, both with severe damage. The house was repairable but the church beyond help. We had to start from the ground up on it, and as supplies were scarce, and deliveries to the area few and far between, we believed we were there to build, and that was our focus. They had dumped some lumber and steel rebar on the site, prior to our arrival, so we set to work, to go as far as materials would allow. Every day from the beginning, we used up everything supplied, so on returning to our shelter for the night, we voiced our list to our leaders, and they told us they had spoken to suppliers, but always, either trucks were unavailable, or supply barges had not arrived yet, so we waited for morning. In the morning, we ate together early, and while we ate, we were led in a devotional, by Arnie, a wise, elderly, gentleman, from our group. He would guide us away from our concerns of what we would get in the way of supplies that day, to, a dedication of ourselves, to do whatever would come along, so as not to waste our time there, but to be useful, in whatever way we could. At the end of every twenty minute devotional, he would lead us in a prayer, thanking GOD, for supplying ALL our needs, and protecting us through the day. We believed, we were sent here to make a difference, and I would have never ever imagined, what happened. Ever day, I mean EVERY day, we would get to the job site, and something would have or would happen, that just would stun many of us. In our group, there were people, unknown to each other, some of christian faith and some without, but all, amazed, at how GOD worked to supply every need, material or otherwise, just prayed for that morning. One day we had no wood to finish the trusses that we had been building for six days. The wood for us was still on a barge somewhere, and then, a truck would show up, full of what we needed, that had been sent to a wrong building somewhere else, but they didn't have anywhere to store it, so they sent it back to the depot, and they sent it to us, and the same with cement trucks. The cement company told us they were doing a big pour, and would get to us in a week to ten days, even though we were ready for cement, but wood came, so we did the needed wood work. The next day, they had a problem at their big cement pour, the forms broke, so as the trucks were full, with no where to go, guess where they ended up? You got it, all the cement we needed, and yet, we never had any extra, just the amount we required, not two wheel barrel fulls more. It was like that with every thing. We never wasted time, we never sat wondering when or what we would get, we just trusted, and it worked out. None of us was there for ourselves. We were all there for the same reason, to help, and after all was said and done, we had rebuilt the house, built the roof trusses, footings and bottom floor of the church, and built a house for a singe woman and her children. When we had finished our time there, before going our own separate ways, the group was all moved to tears, from what we had accomplished, not on our own, but completely under the guidance and control of GOD. HIS work, HIS timing, HIS strength provided to us, all under HIS protection. We all came away, changed, and blessed more, than those we went to help.

Back at home, we got involved in a property deal, that just happened, that, with a relatively small investment, would show, returns twenty five times greater, spread over seven years, which would save us taxes and worked into our selling the business and moving forward to be available for what would come next. God had a part in all of it.

We felt led to donate to a Bible College in our area, and started a Memorial Trust Fund, in my mothers name, and later added my daughters name, and have pledged to give beyond what we are capable of, and you want to know something, GOD will have a part in that too, and we will give even more, than we could have even promised. I know it!

When I was doing well, making a good living, was nothing, compared with what happened financially, after I started giving back to GOD, what was HIS. I made much more money after I was fifty years old, than all of those good years when I did it all myself, and you know why!!!

10 OUT OF 10 DIE, and, ALL of US, will leave everything we have, behind!!!

CHAPTER 8

Sometimes in life, you come up against people or circumstances, that stops you from helping them, or what they are trying to accomplish, and in the end you figure out, it was because of greed or ignorance, or both! Even if you have the ability and understand how to end up with a positive outcome, your hands are tied.

It was on one day, while sitting in my office, scrolling through my stock portfolio's, one of my customers, I had known for some time, asked to speak to me about an investment, in a local company. It caught my interest, so we sat and I listened to him, explain about this credit counseling company, how it needed financial help, and was a great investment opportunity. As the stock market, was not doing the greatest, I figured, I would get more information, and look at a small investment, in the company. As the company's objective, was to help those in need of reorganizing their finances, and to avert bankruptcy, I felt it would be a viable, direction for improving society in general. The more I learned about all the self inflicted problems the company had, the more I realized, what was needed most, was someone with good business sense, to manage and move the company forward, and after buying some shares, was kept informed of how they were doing on a regular schedule.

One day, out of the blue, the President of this counseling company, phoned me, and asked if he could come and visit with me, in regards to some changes they were making in the company. At the time arranged, the President, Al, arrived and introduced the new President, that was officially taking over the Company, within a few days. I got to know Al, through a few previous meetings, and realized he had some heath issues, and so, him stepping down, didn't seem out of the ordinary. This new guy, struck me as a traveling, vacuum cleaner salesman at first, but during that meeting, he told me, he had been informed by Al, that I had success in turning businesses around, and he would like to meet me on a weekly basis, to help, in the restructuring, and improving the Company, to profitability. As I was always wanting to make a difference, and seeing how I had shares in the Company, how could I say no?

Over the next months, I began to realize, just how bad the Company was really doing. It had annual sales of around 4.5 million dollars, and lost approximately three quarters of a million dollars over the last two years, and for a small company, should have been finished, so that gave me an indication of the viability of such a company. It had the ability to survive on such huge losses, still keep the doors open, still meet payroll, and still paying the management, way too much, for it's size. There was definitely something here to work with, but many hurdles yet ahead. The weekly meetings with the new CEO/ President, turned to daily, and sometimes, took up most of my day. Soon he asked me to join the Company as a Board Member, so I could use my knowledge and my recognition, for the better of the Company. As the Company, had tax debts, pending lawsuits, overdue unpaid bills, and regulatory problems, I told him, I would only dedicate my time as a silent Board member, until those problems were resolved.

Over the next two years, involvement was deeper and more time consuming, but, management was listening to some direction. But there was a major flaw in the system, something I realized from the get go. The Company, had a few hundred shareholders, but they had no represen- tation, anywhere in the Company. The owners of the Company, were the Directors, and all they seemed to care about, was filling their own pockets, through their nice salaries, and bonus structure. They sold off all these shares, to friends, family, just about anyone, but they never lost any share control as they sold them off. So at the end of the day, the Company took in money from selling of shares, the money went into the Company to pay the bills, of which, management fees and expenses, were a large portion, and the management still owned eighty percent of the shares. Oh, the employees of the Company, were working their butts off, and money was coming in, but the share sales were established, to pay down debt, which never happened, so the financial situa- tion never improved. When the new CEO/President was brought in, the existing President and Vise-President, who owned eighty percent of the shares, agreed to give the new President one quarter of each of their shares and return one quarter to the Company, but then, I think they realized, they would not control the Company if they did that, so they hired the new President's, brother, as Vise President, and gave him the other twenty-five percent, free, just so they would not lose control. This didn't come out until years later.

It didn't take me long to figure, "GREED" was the biggest denominator in this chain of command, so I set to work, to come up with a plan, to dismantle their share structure, to gain control of the Company, and return it to the proper shareholders. The previous Auditors, had a huge outstanding bill, for work done over the years, and they were suing to collect, but, having done the books, they knew, there was nothing for them, so I agreed, to buy their debt, pay them directly, thirty cents on the dollar, but take the full amount of debt from the Company, in shares. This, relieved their debt, and their lawsuit, released their books, and put me in a ten percent owner- ship, share position, while at the same time, keeping the Company from claiming bankruptcy.

Next, was a time consuming, and long series of events, that made it possible, to accomplish what I set out to do. The Board, consisted of, the CEO/President , his brother as Vice President, and the previous Vice President's wife, who was there to represent his position of ownership, while he still was employed, by the Company, as the Sales Manager. I was added to the Board, along with another outside Director #2, responsible for shareholder representation. It didn't take too long, before there was fur flying between myself and the CEO's brother, as I ended up in the Board position of, Chairman of the

88   JERRY TEMPLETON

Compensation Committee, and had to set negotiations standards, for the management salaries, going forward. I established, base salaries, with performance bonuses relating to the Company sales and profits, and then, those bonuses, were paid in share options, so as to save the cash flow, in order to pay down the Company debts. Over the next year and a half, the Company teetered on cash short positions, and through sales of limited amount of shares, got them through some dangerous times. During one of the tight cash periods, without disclosing it, the president's brother, used restricted funds, from the government restricted "trust fund", and jeopardized our business license. Due to that mistake, the Board, pressured the Chairman of the Board, to fire his brother, the Vice President, in order to salvage our business license, and help to give us some time, to raise a bit more cash through share sales. He was to get no severance pay, and was to be removed from the Company immediately, and that is when we found out he had been given the few million shares free, when he joined the Company, by the previous management. Well, as it was his brother, the CEO ended up paying him for the next 4 months, against the Board's direction. A big mistake!

Six months later, I had been in communications with the other two Board Members, regarding the actions of the President/CEO, with regards to a number of issues. Not only had he paid his brother on leaving the Company, but he had hired a Consultant, to take the Company public, or somewhere, to get it out of debt. It was on the edge of bankruptcy again because it was out of compliance, with the government business practices agency. The Chief Financial Officer(CFO),and the Chief

Operations Officer (COO), both were concerned about what the CEO was doing, so through phone conversations, I told them to refuse to return to work under the CEO. I then called a emergency Board Meeting, with one Board Member in Las Vegas, and the other in Manitoba, Canada. I informed them both of what was and would happen, and informed the CEO, we were going to lose our license, which was the truth. Only him and I were in the room, with the other Board Members on speaker phones. When the meeting was called to order, I took the floor, and much to the CEO's dismay, started reading his letter of resignation, and putting a motion forward, for him to sign it and all to accept it or his second option, I also had a letter on the table, to fire him, it was his choice. He sat there, stunned for a bit, until it sunk in! He had no choice, but to save face, sign the resignation letter, and walk away, having done his best with the flailing Company. Signed, sealed and done!

Next step, was, to find someone, other than myself, to run the Company. Their are three different types of CEO's required to build a company. First there is the set up guy. He starts the company, sets it in motion with all the needed requirements, licenses etc. to get it working. Then there is the turn-a-round guy. He takes over for the one that gets it going but can't get it working properly, as he isn't skilled enough to make it successful. He makes the required management changes, financial arrangements, and contractual obligations, to move the Company, to a profit building position. Usually his skills are limited to turning and not to growing it. Next comes the finisher. It may not be the final CEO, but he will have the skills needed to grow the Company, now with financial health.

That requires staff and management health, with a focus on relationships, long term employee's, and solid, achievable, growth budgets, with governance and finances in place, to allow all focus on growth. This position, can take the first CEO, to grow sales from 5 million to 20 million, next CEO, 20 to 100 million and so on.

As we had a Consultant hired, we though, the best thing would be, to use him for the turn-around position, and as he had informed us he already had a financial backer in place to move forward, we started negotiations for him to stay on. We didn't know him, and any info we tried to find on him was sketchy, but we ended up giving him a very hefty compensation, as he threatened to pull his financier if we didn't. He was a short fuse, with total disregard for anyone that got in his path, and played the odds on going to court after every move he made. So over the next one and a half years, he cleaned house. I met with him every week, we called each other almost every day, no matter where I was. We had a close relationship, and the Board worked hard to keep us out of the courts, due to his path of destruction. We now had a board consisting of, the CEO, CFO, Director #2, and myself, and soon replaced the #3 Director, the ex V.P.'s wife, with another outside Director, so going forward, the Board would be governed by more outside Directors, than Management.

Refinancing, was a challenge! The new Consultant/ CEO, threatened to pull the financier off the table if the Board didn't sign a GSA (guaranteed security agreement), which he said was required, as, the old management, could jeopardize the financial arrangement, due to the amount of shares they owned. If they threatened, which they were doing, with the GSA, he could fold the Company, and it was agreed, it would be restarted for a dollar, with all previous shareholders, minus previous "trouble" management, and without debt load. It was also agreed, the GSA would only be used if the previous management, was to take actions to destroy the Company, and that was the only understanding which the Board agreed to sign. Two of the three Board members signed, with Director #2, refusing to. When the refinance deal came down, at first the CEO wanted to roll back all the shareholders at 100 to1, and we fought back and said, no way! We finally agreed, the shareholders that invested in the Company, including the Directors, would take a 10:1 rollback and previous management, that got the company into trouble would have to agree to a 20:1 rollback, along with a share trust agreement, that would lock their shares into a voting trust agreement, voted by myself. And who, you might ask, would sell this rollback to everyone, especially the 20;1 to the old management? Who else! They hated and would not talk to the new CEO. They didn't trust the CFO. They didn't have much experience in dealing with Director#2, so I was elected, and Director #2 assisted the deal completely. There were some very heated discussions, some serious threats, last minute change of minds, but we stayed the course, never were intimidated, and in the end, we convinced them all, it was our way or they would lose everything. We played on their GREED. And that was the deal. The Company went from 35 million shares to 3.4 million, including the new shares sold to help raise some extra funds as requested by the financier. We now had a manageable company, with still a bit of house cleaning left.

IT was after the CEO's 16th month, when after court cases, a sexual harassment payout, and removal off most former management, he felt threatened by the Boards directive. That would put the Chief Operations Officer (COO), in charge of business, and have him separate himself from day to day operations, so he could concentrate on the bigger picture of growing the Company. He then set about, to get rid of the COO, that had been there for three years, and reported regularly to the Board. He said he had a workout agreement, signed and in place, to set up and get rid of, the COO. He LIED! We talked privately with the COO. She was a smart and honest woman, and she knew what he was up to, and as she had seen how he operated, and didn't trust him, recorded all his memo's to her, kept all his email, and directives, and showed the Board. She had a solid case that would cost us dearly if we went to court against her. So, we challenged him to produce the signed contract, and he looked, but couldn't produce it, so from that moment on, he did everything in his power, to try to get rid of the Board Members. He went into the Directors, private emails, made copies of them, tried to use one Director against another, threatened staff on communicating with the Board Members, even threatened to take the Directors to court and to take the Company into receivership, but we didn't give in to his rantings. We worked with the Financier, and acquired legal opinion, to make sure everything that was done, was reported properly, and demanded contractual obligations be met by management through guarantees given by them, on the signing of the refinance deal. So, even though, the CEO didn't communicate to the board, we still had meetings, and still had financial reports weekly, through the financier. During this "blackout" period, we established through many heated emails and nasty threats from the CEO, new "Governance Policies", that had even more stringent controls in place by the Board. Even though the CEO, thought sticking his head in the sand would save him from answering to the Board, it was really his undoing. During this period, we also did reviews for his contract extension, which, after concluding, we gave him notice of end of contract. With a CEO review done by the outside Directors, a summary of management fees, prepared by a third party company, followed by a settlement offer. In the end, we removed him from the Company, and, that ended up a huge savings to the Company.

No one had any idea of what was going down, during the removal of the CEO, even the Management was kept from realizing it, until the papers were in front of the outgoing CEO. At that same time, we had a representative from our Financier, deliver a signed letter to the CFO, from the Board, informing him of the change of leadership. He was asked if he would step in as "acting as President" through the remainder of his contract, which was seven months, with a compensation adjustment and a performance bonus tied to budget. It was explained to all the management, that the turn-a-round period was over and now we were in the harvest mode, and that put responsibility on each manager to produce from each of their positions. Immediately, everyone in the Company, took a huge sigh of relief, took the directive from the Board, supported the changes, and set out to move forward it a positive direction, feeling the ability now, to do their jobs.

His reaction, to getting caught, is what I have for years, referred to as, "The President Clinton Syndrome"! It is very common, in reactions from persons, that don't trust anyone, including themselves. The basis is," IT IS ONLY WRONG IF YOU GET CAUGHT, AND, IF YOU GET CAUGHT, TAKE DOWN THE ONE THAT CAUGHT YOU, TO DESTROY THEM BEFORE THEY DO ANY MORE DAMAGE TO YOU"!

It works like this. The soon as you are caught, saying or doing something, that is wrong, or they know they got "caught"at, they immediately turn the tables, usually on the person that found them out. They try to accuse that person, of worse wrong doings than themselves, trying hard to discredit the individual, attacking anything they have ever said, and trying to make it look as if they are just trying to make a name for themselves. They try to take on the "poor innocent me " attitude, but all the time, orchestrating a full blown attack, as if in some way, making them clean. They work at getting everyone to believe, this person has been "out to get them" and really have made their life miserable. Sort of the same lines as the "paparazzi's" fault. They chased me and I was trying to get away from them, so I did all this bad stuff I am now accused of doing, but I had no choice, because they made me do it. Ha Ha. We have heard different variations and will for years to come. It is always someone else's fault. You hear it every day in the news, and all around the world, and as time evolves, the "its only wrong if you get caught" foundation of guilt, suddenly can be used to excuse just about everything going on, that is secretive. It allows reasoning, as a replacement for good judgment and guilt. A dangerous exchange.

Because Bill Clinton got away with using this system, in the highest public forum, suddenly, people from all walks of life, that once had some solid principles, decided, if the President of the United States, can work this unique system, so can they! So now, when you deal with individuals, who believe they deserve a break, just because they think they are smarter than the next, and use this principal, you are most likely dealing with a time bomb of fury, in waiting, almost desiring, that someone come along, and release them from the prison of deceit they have built around themselves. And, sooner or later, they will get exposed, so they are ready, and you must also be prepared. The defense is simple. Honesty! It will always prevail, but, you must never feel defeated by sticking with the truth, and not get distracted by the attack on you as an individual. That is where the breakdown takes place. As long as conversation stays on the wrongdoing, that person will be exposed for what they are. As soon as you start trying to protect yourself, you fail to keep all eyes on whatever you exposed that was wrong. Another, simple lesson, in life's ever changing playground.

And, about that company, remember how it got into trouble? Greed! Well, a couple of years later, the refinancing company, that originally loaned us one million dollars, over five years, was repaid two million dollars. That was their agreement, with one small "fine print". When the company had to pay off the former CEO, they agreed we could skip a couple of payments of principle , and just pay the interest. What was NOT said, was, that ended up, legally putting us offside with the original contract. That would end up giving them 75% of the company, even after paying them back the two million.

More greed! But it didn't stop there. We went to court to try to keep the company, and offered them another two million dollars to buy them out. They wanted seven million!! GREEDY!!! Well, they took over, got rid of the Board, and five years later, the company closed, lost everything. They didn't know how to operate it. SAD. We all lost our investment, and they never got any money to speak of. All because of Greed.

Greed destroys companies, people, and families, especially at time of loss of loved ones during Estate dispersion time. It also ruins health, as it smolders and eats you up inside. Greed! Greed! Greed!! Never good, and always has negative results!

CHAPTER 9

WARNING!! This chapter may include
some "tongue in cheek" remarks!
Please read it in context!

We failed! At least that is the impression you would get if you tuned into one of the many, woman's talk shows on TV. From their view, it looks like the "feminist movement" has taken over, just like they wanted. But wait a minute. Us men didn't have a problem with the " burning the bra campaign", actually, we thought it was a great idea, not even sure who suggested it to start with, probably a guy, but give him a pat on the back. Next, the women wanted our jobs, and many of them moved into those roles. But lets be honest about the whole thing. Men were sick of working, didn't mind women in most workplaces, and most were more than happy, that suddenly, the women's so called equal rights, turned into two family incomes. The sad part is, the fight for equal rights for men and woman, "same pay for same work", never really got finished, leaving a significant difference, in the pay rates for the two sexes. It also set the stage for more divorces, because, as the woman got the independence they went after, they discovered what the men knew all along, and that was, the satisfaction you would get from working your butt off, was over-rated. The money you made, just cost you more to make, drove the cost of living up, and left you with the feeling, you deserved a break someday, but truth be told, the break lasted way too short, for the price you had to pay.

So, that didn't work as planned, so then, the women, felt as if they were tricked into working, and us men, were happy just to be in control of the TV remote, and that was enough responsibility. So that was made into a joke, but we still had the remote, and even belittling us with it, was not going to get us to put it down. So, they had to come up with something better, and guess what they gave us? Male menopause! There you have it. Symptoms of, "grumpy old men", indecision, becoming easily frustrated, having hot sweats, running off with younger women, the list takes on new releases, every week. So lets break it down.

Grumpy old men, comes by from life and all its curves. You work hard, starting when you are young and fit, and you give the best of what you would ever be, and, most men, realize they will never reach the success they thought they had hoped for, in their lifetime. They are constantly challenged by inflation, progress, and time. Those are all against them. Many are disillusioned from day one, that their wife would do everything they could to satisfy them, support them, and make their lives easier.

In way too many cases, that was far from the truth, and many times, that alone led to disappointments, on both sides. I always said, the toughest things on a marriage, were sex, finances, health and family. Usually if you had trouble with any one of these, you usually ended up with another one, as a bonus, tag on, problem. Example, trouble with sexual relationship, causes stress, leads to poor sleep habits, ends up health issues, or financial disaster, when you divorce. Have finance issues, like lack of money to meet your bills, and your sex life will take a beating, and even your heath will suffer from stress. Any of them lead to stress, that nobody seems to be able to remedy. That is, unless you trust and believe in a higher power, GOD that is. That summarizes just how easy it is, for men to get grumpy.

"Can't make up or minds", has been around for some time, and given the responsibility, to treat our wives properly, we slowly learned, that "if mamma wasn't happy, no one was happy". If we made the wrong decision, we were in trouble, if we didn't make any decision, we were in less trouble, so natural recourse, was to take the path of the lesser trouble. That evolved as women ended up in the workforce, turning indecision, into a prerequisite, for a happier household. When the men would come home from work all stressed out, they would usually vent the soon as they walked in the door, in answer to "how was your day honey?" They would have their supper, and grab the remote, tired from a hard day, and now hope to be soothed by their loving spouse. When both are working, it gets to a place, where neither partner, wants to know how the others day went, at least not until you have had time to check on their attitude. This started the great lack of communication process, that followed right behind, equality. Next step, lack of sex, and so the steps follow the cycle downward. Now if you throw a bit of men's history of health in the mix, you can now understand, how directly, that ties to prostate problems, beer belly syndrome, and something that started early in marriage, selective hearing. Sounds like change of life to me. It is just like the old question, what came first, the chicken or the egg?

When it comes right down to it, frustration may have evolved, from woman. We learned it. All the "lazy husband", "good for nothing", "am I the only one around here that can do anything around here?","all you do is flop down on the couch and wait for dinner", and " a woman's work is never done!", finally rubbed off. But how else could we respond to those frustrations expressed. Think about it. If we would have changed, to improve the complains aimed at us, women know how to turn that into a long running victory of sorts, that would include a never ending list of changes they would like to see in us. After all, haven't you heard, you can never please a woman, at least that is what we got from our fathers. So again, the events that change men, took a while, and required, as usual, more serious evolution to men. It never is a simple process. Picture this in your mind, to follow the development. First, because you could never please a woman, and you showed signs of having trouble making decisions, the next step, was predetermined, if you intended to live in close proximity. Loss of hearing, or more precisely, selective hearing. Learned at an early age, and told so by your mother, and from your father, it seemed to be more controllable as you aged. You could hear the coffee wagon turn onto the street, a block away, hear every detail about a football or baseball game, come to think about it, every sport on TV, in a room full of kids, relatives or buddies, but driving along, with just your wife in the car with you, you miss every word she said. That take skills you can't get overnight, so, as I said earlier, it is definitely, evolution.

Just thinking of all the changes men have had to put up with, makes me sweat, so you can just imagine, the reaction to those changes, their body would have to go through. Tie that, to understanding better and better, the older men get, of where in the food chain they actually were, and you have ensured sleeping was a hit and miss opportunity. You work all day, eat too much, too late, fall asleep right after dinner, snore and wake yourself up, and then are expected, to have a peaceful night. Wrong, your mind won't allow anything of the sort. It has full control of your body when you crash for the night, demanding something to drink midway through your snoring, and if that is not enough, as you age, so does your partner, and she has to go through all her monthly, yearly, lifetime changes, that turns the honeymoon bed, over time, into a war zone. The results, you now displease her more, you fit into her categories she has preset for you, handed down from the daytime talk shows, and that confirms for her, your failure as her partner. That must be the icing on the cake.

Most men, end up with some hobby, usually something they can do, out of earshot of their wife. Of course, the older they get, the more relaxed the hobby is, at least for most men. But there is an exception to everything, and men are no different. Some guys, first of all, don't want to admit they have any problem, because they heard all along, ever remark made to them. It sat in their minds, and festered, and in time, showed up in their attitude, their love life, usually had some sort of health, side effects, sometimes even financial ramifications, but in the end, the grass looked greener. It is easier to leave than fight, and my opinion after seeing so many relationships end in breakup, is, if you leave once, it is that much easier to leave the second, and third time. Grass may be greener, but seasons change, and sooner or later, the grass has to take some time off, or be reseeded or fertilized, or it all becomes anything but a nice and green and dies. That is why I have concluded, men enjoy golf so much. No matter what your age or status in life, you can start every game, like is is the best round you will ever have. You can get mad, scream, holler, and even throw your club, and the game will frustrate or reward you. But no one really cares about what you do, unless you win money from them, and the next time out, you get to start from a perfect score again, and work to ruin it. How good is that. And best of all, no one you will ever play with, is ever going to be perfect at it. It just is meant to be that way. A perfect game, that you will never win at, but the chance is always out there waiting, and tempting you, to try. Interesting isn't it, a lot like life.

Well, maybe just maybe, those talk shows hit on something, that is bigger for most of us to fully understand, and maybe, because of what we see our wives go through as they battle their way through the tough change most of them are dealt, it is best for us to ignore those nasty titles. It just is not manly, to be dressed in male menopause, or one or the other handles they have tried to disguise it under. The plain truth, must be, we just got sick and tired, of not living up to the expectations, put on us, as we wrestled with all the curves, life threw at us, and still does. Yup, that's it all right! I don't think there is any lesson to be learned here, do you? Wrong! There is an important lesson!

When I turned thirty-five, I had reached all the goals I had set when I first got married at the age of twenty-one. Our house was paid off, we had cash and investments, making a very good living, had time for holidays somewhere warm for just the two of us in winter months, and time with the kids for summer holidays. Life was good, and it seems to be true, the more money you make, the more you spend. We always had saved money as a priority, and invested it so it would be accessible, while still earning interest. But from then to about age 55, I knew I was always going through some sort of change, physically, mentally and for sure emotionally. Of course some of the changes were brought on by lifestyle of living the good life, which we certainly did, and the physical side was less and less, as was participation in other activities, like baseball, and hiking. Many things also are at work, changing the way you though about or failed to think about some things. Friends ended their marriages, some changed partners, and more of our friends, seemed unhappier about their lives, which all factored into my thought life. I remember, thinking about a few guys I knew, that ran off with younger women, and also throwing me a curve, was when a very close friend, ran off for a while, then came back to his wife and family. Later, he called it, "his other life" and would only explain to me, he just couldn't take it any more, and in the end, missed the family he had, so that, was enough for him to return.

As my wife went through the chemical and mental changes, which started when our three daughters, got married, all within nineteen months, it was if I was watching through a window, as it seemed, there wasn't much I could do. But sooner than later, I came to the full realization, I was in the mix. It felt like I was the target. The more I asked how I could help, or innocently asked how she was doing today, the more nervous I got, about which direction our relationship was headed. The though of ever starting over with a younger woman, would bring me back to the process we went through during those years, and scared me away from wasting any time thinking about it. Those were some tough days, and nights were even tougher. I was afraid to sleep in the same bed some nights, and more afraid, not to sleep in that bed on others. Every day was a challenge for her, and a challenge for me, but, the toughest, was for us. I think during those times, I was also going through changes, and that on top of the frustration with my partner, would have finished us off as a couple, but for a few factors. First, I had some good friends that I could talk to, both male and female. Second, we had great daughters that were starting families, and that was huge, but really, most important, was my belief and trust in GOD. My brother, during that time, although younger, put up with my frustration, and although he didn't solve my problems, he was always an ear that I filled. My wife and I never were the same after, as before, but I think that is also part of the whole process, as you don't want to stay the same. As you reach that time in life, your needs and priorities change, and you continue to put different value on things, as you go forward more together from that point.

After my father passed away, my wife insisted I go to see my doctor, for regular checkups. Just before my fiftieth birthday, my PSA tests were a way too high, so for the next ten years, as the numbers climbed, so did my anxiety, not to mention the changes it made to my sleep habits and grumpiness level. During that time, I went through two needle biopsies. The last one, ending up giving me a serious infection, that knocked the wind out of my sails for a couple of months. During that whole process, my doctors insisted I must have cancer, although I had no symptoms that would back those feelings up, but all the time, mentally fatigued by the "not knowing". I went to California and paid for a P.E.T. Scan, which showed "no cancer" anywhere, and had more tests done, all to prove what my Doctor told me before we got married. I had an oversize prostate! Following that ten years, and ending up with good results, I retired and spent lots of time doing those things we had planned on doing, when we had those "newlywed plans" for our life. But those tests, brought me to a reality check, and got me more focused on putting good health, on the top of the list. Again, all roads to good health, pointed to controlling the "stress level" in ones life.

So, to the issue of male menopause, I reflect, it should be called " male re-evaluation" or "male refocus". I believe it is a necessity, for men to re-evaluate and refocus, as to goals they believe they can still accomplish. Get rid of those unattainable ones that ended up as just dreams. Set some future priorities, along with revisiting some of those dreams you shared with your spouse. That will make you younger again, when you revise and finally live them in real time. To learn the lesson of being older, but remembering the dreams of when you were younger, and putting them back into a "work in progress" folder, will help you through your changes.

CHAPTER 10

You have had to of heard of "The Power of Positive Thinking", through some book or some speaker somewhere, as there have been numerous persons remark on that statement. It is true! I have had that attitude for most of my life. Not always in the right direction and I am sure it was not always for a positive outcome for anyone but myself, but over the years, I have realized, how really important, that attitude really is. It has helped in my relationships, helped in making new friends, and helped me huge, in dealing with tough things I have had to deal with in life. It removed many of the stresses that tried to rob me of a good nights rest, allowed me to help others, which in turn, makes you feel better all around, and gave me a better platform mentally, from which to make important decisions. I think I had that positive attitude already when I was young, long before I ever heard it from Robert Schuller Senior, and "The Hour of Power" on television. My mother had that same attitude, saying things like "if you can't say something nice, don't say anything at all" or " do unto others as you would have them do unto you" or even, "ever time you help someone, you are helping yourself"! Never could fully understand the full value of those quotes, then. Reality is, life improves 100%, effort is reduces ten fold and all of it results in you ending up, a better person. The bonus part is, life is so much easier and more fulfilling. Mom also used to tell us, it was easier to smile than to frown, and she read somewhere it even took fewer muscles do do so, not to mention it gave you less wrinkles in the end.

In my business, I often spent time, talking, or mostly listening to my customers as they waited for their vehicle to come out of the shop. Because I showed a positive attitude, it sort of drew them to me, and I always made myself available. It made my days go by quickly and I always felt like I had made a difference in their lives. It opened my eyes to how most other people had to live, gave me a different perspective. Sometimes all I would do is share my experiences with others, sometimes, give them financial advice, other times, just supported what they were trying to accomplish, without even telling them how. It is amazing, how many strangers, just needed some positive re-enforcement in what they plan on doing. No need to scold or direct them, just pat them on the back and say "good for you , great idea", "give it your best effort and you will succeed"! Many times, through listening, I would end up with a pretty good idea, that a bit of a help financially, would make a fantastic difference in their life, and many times I did, even though it was never asked for or expected. I would tell them everyone needed a break sometime, as I had many in my life, and it was no obligation to them. I asked nothing in return, just the satisfaction of knowing it could be the difference between them making it or not. Sometimes I would get letters or cards back, occasionally they would drop in at a later date to inform me of their progress, and sometimes, I would never hear from them again, and that was OK too, because that is what I told them they could do. I didn't want any credit, nor any feeling they owed me. The good feeling was in the ability to allow them to continue on through their own life, but with a bit of a boost.

One day, a young woman brought in her car that was making lots of noise. I had the crew check it out and found it needed $800. worth of work, just to drive it back out of the shop. The brakes were shot and the exhaust was broken in two. While they were looking at it, I sat and talked to her in the waiting room. Her and her husband had a one year old son, only married a couple of years, and she had just been diagnosed with breast cancer. He was working night shift and really struggling, not only financially, but she said he was really struggling with her having cancer. She was just a small woman, about twenty six years old and she asked me if we could just fix her car enough to drive it for a few months while she underwent surgery and treatment. They were planning to move back with her parents in another town, so they could help with their baby while she went through the treatments. When the estimate came in, she just sighed, as if to give up. She said they couldn't afford to fix it, so she would talk to her husband to figure out what to do next. I could see she felt totally defeated. Totally! I told her that I would have her driven home and picked up the next morning and her car would be ready to go. She reiterated they only had a few dollars and could not afford the repairs. I told her not to worry, we would work it out. Next morning, we picked up her and her husband and their little boy. Her husband was close to six feet tall, approximately twenty four, and looked like he came along to keep his wife from getting ripped off. He never expected what happened next. They came up to the counter, and I handed them the bill, and their car keys, and said, "NO CHARGE"! I told them the bill was just for warranty, and they needed a break, they had enough on their plate, so this was on the house, our gift to you both! Well, that six foot guy, with his old lumberjack shirt and old blue jeans on, never saw that coming! Those tears running down his face would not stop. I walked outside with them, to their car, and he just kept saying he didn't know how to pay me back. I told him he never would have to and I never expected anything in return, just wanted them to work hard to get her healthy again. We hugged, he still had tears, and they drove off together. I never saw them again, knew we had helped in a big way, and actually, I think I felt better that they did!

I have discovered, there are two very distinct and totally opposite results of the two attitudes to life. Stress has an inward direction of destruction, which as it festers ends up effecting your health in a negative outcome. Positive thinking, does the exact opposite and gives you better quality of life. When I was in high school, I had a business teacher that spent a number of years in Japan and ended meeting his wife there. During his time overseas, he started to get involved with Japanese martial arts with the use of mind over matter. He taught me after class, about some of the reasoning and methods of training he went through. One such training, was a extension of, how the body reacts in time of stress, to parts of the anatomy. If for example, you had a serious cut to one hand, the body, sensing the damage, would immediately respond by sending extra blood flow to the injury, and taking it from other parts of the body that were normal. This normally will result in lightheadedness, or fainting, so the body would drop to a flat or prone position, so it didn't have to work so hard to pump the blood around, and the parts of the body it stole blood flow from, wouldn't notice it. Well, he taught me the extended principle, of mind over matter, that would allow you to concentrate on lowering blood flow to one hand, and increasing it to another. It is all in the concentration, but you can see the results within minutes of the exercise. The hand you concentrate on, swells and turns red, the other, shrivels and goes white. It is amazing how fast you can learn to control it. Of course, they push it to the limits, use it for making body parts stronger that others, to allow it to take a beating, as in breaking bricks, all the way up to, helping ones self, overcome sickness and health issues.

On the other hand, stress, robs you of your ability to think straight, reason things through with a clear mind and effects your whole being. Depression, feeds on negative energy, multiplied many times over by disrupting a good nights rest, ruining your digestive system with acid buildup, and attacking common sense. The further you fall into those symptoms, the worse your heath deteriorates, and the circle of a downward spiral continues. Depression is extremely devastating to not only yourself, but everyone near and dear to you, as it is a deep internal disorder, which controls the mind more, as it consumes the health of the body.

The Japanese art form resembles the way positive thinking works. It takes positive powers and through the thought process, uses them to take your mind away from your own problems. It resembles, seeing someone really poor and living below anything you would consider reasonable, and then realizing how good you have it. That is the principle, many fundraisers and charity organizations use to get people to donate. That is not a bad thing, as it is good for us to make a difference, to better others lives. It makes you feel good inside. And that is the power part, in "the power of positive thinking".

Another small but deadly item on the list, that ruins the chances for achieving the rewards connected to positive thinking, is holding a grudge or not forgiving someone. If you carry that grudge, more than a few hours, or can't find it in your yourself to forgive someone, for saying, doing or whatever against you, you are the one that will actually be the loser. Understand, that in a positive attitude, there is no room for negative. It will ruin and drain, the good feeling ,and replace it with frustration, built up anger, and cause unnecessary stress, and thus the cycle restarts. Forgiving, usually will be required sooner or later anyway, so realizing this sooner than later, will give you a head start, and not rob your positive energy. Such a simple reminder, of just how easy it is, to get off base, and open your thought process to stress, or not! It is totally in your control!

The story of the little train trying to pull his heavy load up the hill, and kept saying "I think I can, I think I can" is a simple but very real life lesson. If you truly want to succeed in anything you do here on earth, believe it. You can spend a lot of money learning how to do things, but if you believe you can do anything you put your mind and energy into, YOU WILL SUCCEED! If you sell yourself with the attitude you can, you will have the confidence, visible to all, that you are going to make it happen. If you stop and look really close at some of the people in the world, that really do make a difference, and are successful, you will notice, everyone stops and listens to what they have to say, and you will also discover, they all have that same desire and commitment. Oprah Winfrey is one of those woman, that just will never be fully satisfied with all the great and wonderful things she will accomplish during her lifetime, and she will never stop working hard to do them all. The challenge is, the more she gives and does, the more she sees she can, and that just continues to drive her. But anyone can do the same thing, if they give themselves fully without any doubt. Oprah didn't start at the top. Most successful people, started at the bottom, never took no for an answer, and most important, never gave up. History shows, those that made the biggest difference, took big risks, but gave it all they had. Start small, give it your best and more, and you too can see the fruits of an all out effort, and accomplish things that someday will amaze you, by where you will be. THINK POSITIVE!

CHAPTER 11

The chapter I never wanted to write!!

YOUR CHILD HAS CANCER!!!!! You die inside! From the moment you hear those words! And you just keep dying, at least that's how you feel! You cry from the depths you didn't know existed in your being, then you moan and cry some more. The biggest and toughest challenge we ever had to face in our life. It was October 29th. The day we forgot what a good nights sleep was! I thought I had lived my life with all it had to throw at me until that day!

My wife and I had just arrived in Hawaii for a month long vacation at our timeshare. It was in a remote part of the Big Island, near the Volcano. The first day there, we decided to hike down to the ocean on the old lava flows, to a remote area with a sandy beach, forty feet below the lava fields. We spend a fantastic day together and enjoyed the hike, the beach, the lava and it's caves, and the spectacular views, and ate our picnic lunch we had taken with us. As we started back to the car, about a one hour hike, my cell phone rang with a call from our daughter, but when I answered it, I could not get a strong enough signal, so missed the call. We got back to the car and started the one and one-half hour drive back to the condo, but stopped a few minutes after leaving the lava, to buy some local fruits at a small homemade stand with a young boy, in the middle of nowhere. When we got back in the car I saw there was a good cell phone signal, so I returned the call to our daughter. She sounded very nervous, and told us she was with her sisters, and the reason she called. Her doctor had just informed her she had cancer in one of her kidneys, and would be going into surgery to remove it within the week, and, ,"COME HOME RIGHT AWAY"!!,..all in tears, as were we all!!! She said she was going to pick up her children from school, and for us to call her at her sisters house in a few hours, as she did not want the kids to know anything yet. We were stunned, shocked, numb, dumbfounded, speechless, all at once! We drove in silence, in disbelief, the one and one-half hour drive back, all the while, trying to digest this horrible information.

As soon as we reached our condo, I called Alaska Air, and told them we needed to get home immediately, and explained the situation. The representative,a caring and understanding woman, told us there were no available seats out the next day, but not to worry, just be at the airport by 11 am the next morning, let them know at the booth who we were and the situation, and everything would be arranged already for us to fly home on the first flight out. Even in our state of despair we felt lifted. Then we called our daughters home,,, our three daughters and their husbands, were sitting on the living room floor, overcome with raw emotion, almost out of tears, that is until we called! They had been waiting for our call. We talked and cried for an hour, them telling us everything they knew and what had happened, us telling them we would be home the next evening. I hung up the phone, and cried!!! But that word "CRIED", does not even come close to describing what happened,, it was like every organ in my body was trying to get out through my throat, at the same time, until exhaustion. Never experienced that before or after that day, almost like an out of body experience, every emotion at the same time, just pouring out. We never slept much after that moment, and for months to come.

It would send us in a new direction of challenges, something we had touched on, but never felt the full impact of. The next twenty-four hours to get back to our daughters and their families, drained us mentally and physically. Knowing what they were feeling, without us being there to share their pain of hearing the "C" word so close to home, no, in it actually, was brutal! At the airport around midnight, we literally fell into our other two daughters arms, and cried all over again, this time, with them. The next morning, after the kids went to school, we met at our eldest daughter, Kristin's home, our girls, and Kris's husband, and started from square one. Loving consoling, trusting God, and supporting each other, as we planned what the future had in store, the unknown!

This whole nightmare started with Kristin having pains in her shoulder for two months. At first it was thought to be an after effect from a car accident two years prior, and at first, physio seems to be reducing the pain. Finally they sent her to have a cortisone shot into her shoulder to help the healing process. Just before we left, I remember voicing my concern to her, about how the shot may mask an injury that needs proper attention. Before the sports clinic doctor gave her that shot, he sent her for a scan as a precaution, and in that scan, the lungs came into question. Unknown to her, they called her back before letting her leave, so they could take another scan to clarify what they saw in her lungs, and that showed a small tumor in her kidney. Someone was guiding their concerns, and the surgeon was impressed that someone during that process, actually saw the tumor. In his words, "it was a miracle" they saw something. And we would hold those words close.

Kristin had gone, alone, to see her doctor about the results of her scan, when she was told she had cancer! I still can't believe the doctor had no understanding of the impact that word has, on a forty year old, mother of four, ages six to fourteen, and to let her walk out to her car and drive away. How ignorant! Kristin phoned her sister, and drove to her house, where she called her sister's twin sister and told her to come over right away, before going home from work. They had the house to themselves as they shared the news and cried together, and formulated how to tell their husbands and us, in Hawaii. The men were told to come to the house, and once there, Kristin was allowed to be alone with her husband to explain, and the rest were told in another room. After a while, they all sat together on the floor, and cried and each one took a turn, to pray for each other, their families, us, and the journey, that lie ahead.

When Kristin and husband met with the surgeon, the next day, he told them, he was going to remove her one kidney that had a tumor in it, within the next two weeks, then they would put her on chemo, to address the cancer in her lungs, then radiate the tumor under her shoulder blade. He said it would be a bumpy road for the next year! Kristin was excited, over some good news, as she stated,"I have another year with my children, that's awesome!" She didn't think they were going to give her any time, let alone a year. You have to grasp on to any bit of good news you get, and that is how you get through some of those days that seem long and hopeless. In grasps. One small step at a time.

Nine grandchildren, ranging from six to seventeen in age, all had different understanding levels and a wide range of emotions. Each was told at their level by their parents, separately, so as to allow each the time needed to understand, question and deal with the shock that followed. We felt it was important for them all to know they could ask anything the wanted, and express any emotions they felt, as to ensure they understood, we all felt the same, had the same angry times, same crying moments, and same desperate moments. There was no right or wrong way to feel. We believed God would be by our sides through it all, and give us the strength we needed. We had people praying from so many differ-ent places, family, friends, churches all over, and those prayers, would carry us, like the pictures of footsteps in the sand, but with many footsteps, not just one set! We also, together, agreed it was important to try to keep life as normal as we could for them. They saw us cry more together, and we still laughed, sometimes, but not as often, but it was accepted as part of our lives now. We had always been a huggy family, but now, the hugs meant a whole bunch more, and crying came even more often than ever. Often, during dinner! Whatever was needed, and, by anyone!

Her surgery was booked for November 14th, then changed to the 21st. Meanwhile she had more scans, including a bone scan, ultrasounds, and a mammogram, then another mammogram, due to, whatever, always leaving you wondering, then texting, then reminding each other, we are not in charge. The whole time, Kristin is still having extreme pain in her shoulder, and can' even lift her arm over her head, so they give her more medication, to dull it, and you wonder some more! Oh yes, this all happened in the first ten days after hearing the diagnosis. And, the same week, it was their eighteenth wedding anniversary, their eldest son's fourteenth birthday, and just around the corner, two more of their children's birthdays, and Christmas! Who has time to fit in surgery, recovery and chemo?? Thank you, all those "whoever's", that kept on praying for our family. I don't know how anyone can get through these times without believing in a greater power and an almighty caring God, looking down from above with LOVE, I just can not imagine going it alone!

Kristin had surgery, they removed her left kidney and ureter, they radiated her right shoulder, and we all spent Christmas together, with her recovering, and sharing the celebration with many tears, still in the shock of the reality, and uncertain for the road that lay ahead, starting with chemo in the following weeks.

Kristin started a blog, "canadiankristinconnected@ blogspot.ca", so she didn't have to repeat her journey over and over to her friends. The blog went international and a year later was read by over 190,000 persons, worldwide. She expressed what it was like to fight cancer, the good and the bad, the pain, the love from strangers, friends, and family, the trust in God, every moment of her journey. Many would put their caring and prayers to her and her family, in words that everyone could see and feel. It unveiled so many hearts of love. Her friends started an on line sign-up, that delivered home cooked meals to her home, for her family, that went on for one and one-half years, six days a week. WOW!!! That's a lot of love and effort by a lot of people, to feed a family of six, and keep it from being routine. How do you ever, ever, thank those families for their sacrifice of time and money, Kristin knew how, and we all prayed for those families every day, that God would bless them many times over for their kindness and love.

The second week of January, the chemo started, and a long journey of serious challenges, for Kristin, her husband trying to keep working and loving on his wife through it all, her children, with their disrupted life, school and the rumors they faced from children hearing their parents talk of their mother dying, meals from strangers that didn't know the eating habits and dislikes, and the rest of us, doing our best, full time, trying to fill in the gaps. Although they call it that, chemo is anything but routine.

The next twelve months, we spent our lives trying to live as close to normal as possible for the children, while spending our time, helping to take care of her and her family, her doctor appointments, radiation, chemo, hospital stays, trying to pick up the kids from schools on time, feed them all, school activities, Christmas, birthdays, sleepovers, far from normal. A New Normal! And we never stopped running and never stopped believing she was going beat the disease. Why her ? Why now ? Why ever? Why? Why? Nine months after they discovered the cancer, and after radiation, chemo, painkilling drugs, and lots of tough days, she had a two month break, so we all took a two week family summer vacation, all seventeen of us, like none other, or ever will be, to visit Disney World. A very special friend wanted to help somehow, and paid for Kristin and her family's cost of their flights. WOW! So thankful we had that alone, away from everyone and everything time. As it turned out, it was our only opportunity.

It was only a few months of higher hopes, until the cancer came back with a vengeance. A couple of weeks before Kristin slipped into a coma, her cancer doctor sat us down and told us they had done all the could for her, and there was no more they could do, other than keep her pain level down. Then he went and told Kristin! Two days before her coma, she called in her children and husband, and my wife and I, and as she could not sit up, had her two youngest, lay beside her in her hospital bed, and with her arms wrapped around them told them, the doctor told her she was going to die very soon, and go to be with Jesus. She said they could be mad right then, and cry, and even scream out loud if they wanted to, but tomorrow they would have to be strong for each other and their dad, and be thankful, yes be thankful, for one day they would see each other again, in Heaven. Could not believe my Girl's gentle loving caring spirit of understanding love, as she explained and comforted them, in her last hours. Heart wrenching! A zillion tears flowed in that room, each of us holding onto a child, still amazed at our girl, and an unbelievable mothers love shone through. After a bit, she called in her sisters and husbands, said her goodbyes, prayed for each of them as they would continue on without her, then called in her in laws and family, and did the same with them. Calm tears of love came from her that day, and we got to spend our precious time alone with her too, and by the next evening, she was in a coma.

Kristin Lorraine Erickson (Templeton) was buried, following her memorial service, on February 14 th, Valentines Day, how fitting for Our Sweetheart, two weeks short of her 42nd birthday. A week later, as I tried to grasp the reality of it all, wrote this to all those that were following her blog;-

A DADDY'S HEART

"I will never leave you or forsake you"

That is God's promise to us all if we trust him! And we have felt the prayers of all our friends carrying us through each moment, and know, it won't be long until Kristin meets me at those pearly gates, although, I am in no hurry, nor do I want to leave the rest of my family and friends. The reality is, I will come to that time, sooner than many of you, that

I also will pass away. The only guarantee we have in this world, is death.

After Kristin left us, our hearts were so torn, so ripped apart. My human expression of tears, never fixed my feeling of the vacuum left inside. The friends and relatives loving on me through this time, has cushioned the hurt, yet many times each day, and in the middle of the night, the tears just flow without warning. It is so hard to be up, feel like talking, and for me that is totally out of character, and it is difficult to find the ability to focus on anything very long. To watch tv, Olympics or anything, just has no importance, nor gives me much satisfaction. A bit like living in a fog and unable to assert your mind.

My thoughts go to the past sixteen months, the hard days, but more and more, the good times and memories. And most important, my Family, Kristin's husband, my other Daughters and their husbands, and our nine grandchildren, all trying to handle their emotional roller coaster. It keeps me trying to look ahead, something we have been unable to do in this past. Many Lessons of Life we have learned with Kris, continue to push us to be better, more caring, and most important, keep us from being too busy, yet staying focused on each other, family, friends, and strangers we bump into along our journey. Yes, all our days are numbered, but while we are here, each of us can choose to help make a positive difference, to all we come in contact with, and those we go out of our way to help.

Thank You, to all of you, that took time from your busy lives, to pray for, comfort, feed, give in so many ways, just to love on us in your own special way, we are and feel, so-o-o blessed by you all, and we as a family, have been praying all along this journey, that God would bless each of you in return.

Love Kristin's dad

go to
"canadiankristinconnected.blogspot.ca"
for Her story

CHAPTER 12

As for Me. What do I believe? It is interesting, that the world, stops and recognizes Christmas, both Christians and non Christians alike! The story is told in the oldest proven book in existence, the Holy Bible. And, the world is split on whether to believe and live by it, or not! I was raised learning what it said, about the history of the world, how to live and how to die, and what to expect in both. As I grew into adulthood, I chose my own path, without regards for what I had learned as a child. I knew better, or so I thought!

I learned, I am no better than anyone else, and no more important! God does not love and care about me, more than anyone else. It took me a while to figure out what was taught throughout the Bible, LOVE, the number one ingredient! You have all read it or even may have seen it at a sporting event, "FOR GOD SO LOVED THE WORLD THAT HE GAVE HIS ONLY BEGOTTEN SON"! That was Jesus, and He was for every one of us, and the Love, began at Christmas, and the proof, was His death on the cross by the Roman Authorities of the day. The best part! THAT, was the beginning, as Jesus rose from the dead, right under the noses of the mighty Roman soldiers, the most feared in history.

What all that means, is when we die, and leave this earth, if we believe Jesus died for us and all the things we have done wrong, and rose again, to heaven, we will end up in heaven! That means, I will see my mom, sister Shirley, daughter Kristin, and many others that have gone on before me. All possible, because God loved us that much, and because, I asked Jesus to change the way I think, act and feel, and for forgiveness, for all that I have done wrong. That easy!! And that is His love to us, and that is the only way I will get to see those I love again, forever.

And THAT is what I believe!!

MY FINAL THOUGHTS

Everyone has things come up in their lives that push them to their limits, of knowing what to do or how they will ever get through it. What you do with this book is entirely up to you, but hopefully, you can use some of the many lessons of life that I have already gone through, to save you some grief, in your life challenges, OR, you can forget it all. Your choice. But I hope it will help all that read it, somehow. And I ask, if you would make a difference, and please pass this book forward to someone you come in contact with that is struggling, so these lessons might just help them through their life.

First, remember,,,,,

When YOU realize that life has tragedies
and opportunities that are going to
happen, and YOU accept and learn
to make the best of them, only then,
will YOU get the best out of living!

I leave you with these last most important thoughts and hope somehow they will impact the remainder of your life. Questions! I challenge you to answer or live by them, as it will improve your life in more ways that you may not see right away.........

CAN YOU SIGN YOUR NAME TO THIS DAY?.....AS IT WAS YOUR LAST?....

DID YOU LEAVE AN IMAGE OR REFLECTION OF YOURSELF IN IT?......

DID YOU MAKE A DIFFERENCE IN SOMEONES LIFE ?.. POSITIVE ONE ??

IF NOT, WHY NOT START TODAY,........

AND LIVE EACH DAY THAT WAY........... AND,,,,,,,,,TRUST GOD!!!,,,,,,,

YOU WILL BE THE WINNER!!!!!!!!!!!!!!

Lightning Source UK Ltd.
Milton Keynes UK
UKHW012336170620
365183UK00007B/278